MW01223642

# SMALL
# SHIFTS

### CULTIVATING A PRACTICE OF
### STUDENT-CENTERED TEACHING

## KIM AUSTIN PhD

NEW DEGREE PRESS

Copyright © 2023 Kim Austin
*All rights reserved.*

SMALL SHIFTS
*Cultivating a Practice of Student-Centered Teaching*

ISBN      979-8-88926-928-1  *Paperback*
          979-8-88926-971-7  *Ebook*

# CONTENTS

# Foreword

Hundreds of visitors have come to visit the Palo Alto High School Media Arts program. While the program has been there since the founding of the school, when I arrived in 1984, I changed the pedagogy and direction in a dramatic way that you will read about in this book. Visitors started arriving in the 1990s when there were about seventy students, and the program was growing rapidly.

After the new Media Arts Center was completed in 2014, even more visitors came, from teachers to school board members to administrators to visitors from China, Europe, and the Middle East. They came to see why so many kids wanted to sign up for a journalism course. While they were there, they admired the beautiful two-story, glass-enclosed Media Arts Center—a state-of-the-art media production facility funded by the taxpayers in Palo Alto—that includes a broadcast studio and recording booths. By 2023, the program comprised over 600 students and four journalism teachers.

Visitors saw engaged students at work without a teacher telling them what to do. This really impressed them. They were intrigued by how many students wanted to learn how to write when most would shy away from such courses. While they were there, they took in our large award case with more than fifty national awards the students had earned. They took home copies of our ten student-produced publications and asked lots of questions about how the program worked.

In 1996, one visitor—a Stanford University student—also came to see what the buzz was about, but she came armed with a different set of questions. She asked: How did the students get to be so independent? How did I prepare them for their roles? But this visitor didn't stay for a day. She stayed for a year, interviewing students and me, and observing as I wore a tiny tape recorder in a fanny pack so that she could analyze my teaching.

This was how I first met Kim Austin, the author of this book, who conducted her doctoral dissertation research in my classrooms. Those conversations back in the 1990s—which continue into today—have helped me reflect on my teaching in so many ways. Usually, people don't understand their behavior. They just do it and maybe think about it later. This is true especially for teachers. Why do some lessons work and others don't? Figuring this out is hard.

*Small Shifts* helps educators think about the how and the why and provides a framework and definitions for what student-centered learning is. Kim pulls together ideas from all four corners of the education space.

But she does something more—something most books don't do. Kim invites us to have in-depth conversations about instructional practice, like the ones we were having over coffee. In each chapter you'll find reflection questions on how to support students to lead their own learning and how to create the conditions for their success.

*Small Shifts* helps educators imagine what's possible and think about the small things they can do to put students at the center of their learning (where they really should be, not on the side or silently listening).

If I had a magic wand, I would give every teacher a staff development day to discuss *Small Shifts*. I would also make it required reading in every teacher education program across the country. The stories make the ideas concrete, and the framework helps educators put the ideas into action.

Kim highlights what any teacher can do to empower their students to become their best selves. Paraphrasing Maya Angelou: Students will forget what you said. Students will forget what you did. But students will never forget how you made them feel.

—*Esther Wojcicki, Founder, Palo Alto High Media Arts Program, Cofounder, Journalistic Learning Initiative at the University of Oregon, and Cofounder, Tract*

# Introduction

*We're teaching for the wrong century.*

—ESTHER WOJCICKI

What do you remember from your K–12 education? A favorite teacher? A favorite friend? For me, a standout memory is an overnight field trip in eighth grade. Our biology teacher took us camping in three vastly different environments of Washington state: the prairie, the rainforest, and the desert. We staked out meter plots to analyze soil samples and waded into rivers to collect water. We graphed our data and proudly reported what we learned to our parents when we returned. This wasn't just a fun excursion. It was purposeful, meaningful, authentic, and engaging. I don't remember the specifics. I'm not a biologist today. But it felt real and important.

Fast forward fifteen years to an auditorium where I am observing four high school newspaper editors lead their peers in a review of the paper they had just published. The student editors ask, "What did you all think of page one?" and the group critiques the headlines, the layout, the stories. I look around, but I can't locate the teacher in the room. I was intrigued. I spent a year studying the journalism program as a doctoral student and asking questions: How did the students develop these literacy and leadership skills? What conditions had to be in place for this level of independence? And what did the teacher do to prepare them?

## Toward a Vision of Student-Centered Learning

We are at a crossroads in education and the consensus is that we can do better by our K–12 students. Student-centered approaches to instruction can create that spark of joy in learning for teachers and students. We can tap into our students' interests, engage them in meaningful projects, and prepare them for a changing world. But few have focused on how the adults in the system can create the conditions for student-centered learning. What are the design principles underlying student-centered learning environments? And how does the teacher shift their practice from being the sage at the front to the facilitator on the side?

The old three Rs—reading, writing, and arithmetic—have now evolved into twenty-first century learning skills and the six Cs (critical thinking, communication, collaboration, creativity, character, and citizenship). We now have *deeper learning* (which prioritizes critical thinking and problem solving in interdisciplinary contexts), *project-based learning* (which focuses on inquiry, knowledge-building and real-world problems), and *personalized learning* (which centers student choice and differentiation). All these efforts put students at the center with more agency, interactions, and input on their learning.

Emerging evidence suggests that student-centered approaches to learning can lead to achievement gains over traditional or more teacher-centered instruction (Barron and Darling-Hammond 2008; Condliffe et al. 2017). But for many educators, while the goals are admirable, envisioning what student-centered learning looks like in practice is difficult, in part because most of us didn't experience this kind of learning in our own schooling. We tend to teach how we were taught ourselves. And educators who do share this vision may lack systemic support, materials, and opportunities for collaboration to bring it to life. While we recognize that classrooms and schools need to change to better serve students, it's hard to locate practical resources, in a sea of resources, that help educators design learning environments.

In this book I share examples of what's possible by drawing on a cross-section of grade levels, content areas, and demographics and by providing tools and questions to guide shifts in instructional practice. In the final chapter on teacher-centered learning, I include examples of how we can support teachers in moving toward student-centered instruction.

This book was born of frustration. Why, in so many places, are we still teaching the same old ways, in rows, with the teacher at the front of the room doing most of the talking? Why aren't schools and district systems more supportive of innovative approaches to student-centered teaching?

It was also born out of opportunity. The COVID-19 pandemic forced us to break the mold, to teach in new ways, to "do school" in new ways. Is this the window of opportunity we have been waiting for? Do things have to break for us to truly innovate?

Most importantly, this book was motivated by curiosity. Where are teachers and leaders already breaking the mold? Where, despite so many systemic barriers to change, can we find examples of student-centered learning? And what do we know about how teachers and students are thriving in these new spaces?

Many teachers and schools have broken the rules, ignored the status quo, and forged new ways of learning together. But they are not easy to find. I hope that lifting up their stories will help us envision a new way to educate the next generation. The next generation is certainly demanding more—more engagement, more skillful use of technology, and more opportunities for creativity and change-making. Today's students are increasingly diverse with rich life experiences. They bring a vast array of assets that need to be capitalized on as we make stronger connections between their lives at home and their experiences at school.

Unfortunately, even before the pandemic we observed declining student engagement in school, especially decreasing as students progress through middle and high school. According to the 2016 Gallup Poll, only one in five eighth through twelfth graders feel like they have an opportunity to build on their strengths, talents, or interests in school. Researchers from the Yale Center for Emotional Intelligence and the Yale Child Study Center learned that a whopping 75 percent of high schoolers have negative feelings about school. The nonprofit YouthTruth reports that only half of all students think that what they are learning is relevant to the real world. We know that student disengagement is a predictor of dropping out, delinquency, and substance abuse. Compound this with widespread teacher dissatisfaction. Only 12 percent of teachers say they are very satisfied with their jobs (down from 39 percent in 2012), and many teachers are choosing to leave the profession (Moeller et al, 2020; YouthTruth 2017; Henry 2011; Will 2022; Learning Policy Institute 2022).

But we have an opportunity for both teachers and students to become more engaged by focusing on the joyful parts of teaching and learning. We can strive for those moments when we see students light up with accomplishment, empowerment, and personal expression, and when we see teachers light up as they experience their students' excitement in learning. The truth is that designing instruction with students at the center is more possible than it's ever been. We have a rich variety of resources available at our fingertips, the technology to support students to become authors, bloggers, and filmmakers, and collaborative tools for writing and creating. It's a perfect time to consider how we can shift students' learning experiences to become more meaningful, relevant, and impactful.

## Small Shifts in Instruction

In this book I provide a guiding vision and a set of design principles to illustrate key concepts from educational psychology (now often referred to as "the science of learning") through the stories of everyday teachers and classrooms. We continue to have a wide gap between education researcher and practitioner audiences, each speaking different languages. One goal of this book is to bridge that gap with some cross-cutting, research-based concepts, illustrated with real-life stories of classroom practice.

I did not set out to describe what I often heard the late psychologist Ann Brown describe as "glossy coffins," that is, perfect, golden examples, that no one could attempt—or worse, turn people off with their seeming perfection. We have plenty examples of these. Rather, when I interviewed educators all over the country, in search of bright spots, I discovered something a little more subtle, but very powerful. Most of them had not transformed their practice overnight. They had attempted small, attainable shifts in practice over time—weeks and months—that led to better outcomes. They shifted the topic of a lesson, the pattern of classroom discussions, or the audience for a final assignment. I wanted to understand more about these small shifts in instruction, how these new practices were cultivated over time, and how they impacted student learning.

The stories are presented in a framework of five design principles—all As—which integrate theories of learning from across the field:

- **Agency**: Foster student choice, voice, autonomy, and self-regulation (Chapter 1: Follow the Student).
- **Active Learning**: Create "hands-on" and "minds-on" interactive tasks that engage and build student understanding (Chapter 2: Learn by Doing).
- **Authority**: Support students' development of content knowledge (Chapter 3: Pass the Mic).
- **Authentic Audiences**: Provide opportunities for publishing, real feedback, and connection (Chapter 4: Publish to the World).
- **Apprenticeship**: Scaffold student learning with expert modeling and support (Chapter 5: Play the Whole Game).

Each chapter illustrates and explains these concepts and the instructional approaches that put students at the center of their educational experience.

## Who Should Read This Book?

My curiosity about and passion for education drove me to write this book. For the past thirty years I have been working with educators and developing tools that bridge research and practice. Half of those years have been at the non-profit WestEd in the San Francisco Bay Area. I have learned a lot from working with teachers and observing when attempts at shifting instruction succeed and when they fail. My hunch is that one contributing factor is that education is too fragmented. We have specialists in reading or math, experts in curriculum design and assessment, and guidance for evidence-based instructional practice. Knowing who to listen to is sometimes hard. I wanted to create a unifying vision of high-quality instruction grounded in rich learning experiences, offer a set of lenses to guide strategic planning at a high level, and provide tools to inform decision making at the day-to-day level.

One audience for this book is educators who work with K–12 teachers: instructional coaches, principals, curriculum coordinators, professional learning providers, teacher educators, and teacher leaders. Ideally, a coach or principal will pick this book up and suggest that their staff read it over the summer as the focus of a book study. Each chapter provides a lens on instruction and together the chapters provide a conceptual framework that can inform both individual and school-level efforts. The final chapter on teacher-centered learning is specifically geared toward those who work with teachers.

At the district or state level, this book pairs well with efforts to implement profiles or portraits of a graduate. These profiles typically include aspirational statements about students' cognitive capacities or personal competencies like "a critical thinker," "a responsible collaborator," or "a lifelong learner." While these statements are motivating for a community of educators, they often stall at the point of implementation. That is, at the classroom level, how can we support our students to develop these skills, dispositions, and mindsets?

I hope that K–12 teachers who are looking for a way to connect with these aspirations for their students—or for a way to deepen their practice—will enjoy the stories and the opportunity for learning and reflection. At the end of each chapter, I provide reflection questions to help teachers and teacher educators consider their current practice and consider how we might make small shifts toward student-centered learning in our own settings.

## A Learning Journey

Early in my writing of this book, a light bulb went off for me. I wanted to write this book to experience the opportunity that all students—and we adults as lifelong learners—deserve: the spark and the joy of learning. I wanted to experience all five of the "As" I describe here: I wanted to have *agency* and choose what I was learning about to set my own direction. I wanted to learn *actively* by interviewing amazing and inspiring educators, to make connections and establish myself as an *authority* on student-centered learning so that I could help others realize this vision. Through my Book Creators' course class, I *apprenticed* with excellent editors, authors, and teachers who lifted the veil on the mystery of book writing, broke down the components and made it attainable for me. And the pleasure of an authentic performance for a real *audience*—you the reader—is certainly not lost on me. You hold in your hands the result of my learning journey. I hope these bright spot stories of student-centered learning in action can help to light your way.

John Dewey once said, "Give the pupils *something to do*, not something to learn, and the doing is of such a nature as to demand thinking; learning naturally results." A hundred years ago John Dewey had it right. How can we—finally— make him proud?

# CHAPTER 1

# Follow the Student

*Follow the child. They will show you what they need to do, what they need to develop in themselves, and what area they need to be challenged in.*

—MARIA MONTESSORI

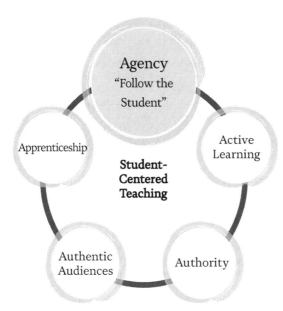

Susan Levenson was stuck. She had been trying all morning to reach a classroom full of high school juniors and seniors who were completely disengaged, staring out the window, at the floor, at their desks—anywhere but toward the front of the room where she was teaching a lesson on essay writing. Finally, it was time for a break, and the students filed out of the classroom. Susan watched through the window as they headed out for a snack at the local taco truck in downtown Stockton. One by one, the students bought their food and then, to her surprise, gave some of their tacos to the unhoused people lining the sidewalk.

When the students returned to the classroom, Susan asked the kids, "How many of you have ever given money to an unhoused person?"

Several of the students raised their hands. She quickly shelved the lesson she had planned and opened a discussion about the housing issue. She asked the students how they felt about giving up their own lunch. One student shared that you can never fully know a person's backstory or where they come from. Another student described his experience living in a car and how people reacted to him differently when they found out he was unhoused. Susan was stunned. Until this point, this student had never uttered a word in class.

Over the next few weeks, with her co-teacher Vickie Lock, Susan quickly developed and taught an inquiry project on income inequality shaped by the students' interest and engagement with the topic. It was driven by the question:

What are the root causes of homelessness and—by extension—poverty? Now the students were hooked. They felt safe in sharing their own stories and were eager to discuss their opinions and conduct research about the income gap in the US.

Susan explains, "The student who shared that day was furious about a lot of things. But it was so real and honest and jarring it just cracked open the room. It kind of took all the stigma out of sharing."

Susan, who is also a colleague of mine at WestEd, has been coaching teachers for decades. She told me her story of coaching and co-teaching with Vickie in an interview. Her words tumbled over each other as she excitedly described the moment they threw their original lesson out the window:

> Our goal was to teach kids to write an essay based on evidence from the text. I didn't care if they learned about giraffes or Pluto. I wanted them to be able to use evidence to inform their own decisions, to be able to understand this tsunami of information that's coming in, to make informed critical decisions about what to process, what to believe, and what to use and then how to use it.

Vickie had tried so many things but according to Susan, "She hadn't really given herself permission to just *turn it upside down*" and drop the intended lesson on the law. The stakes couldn't have been higher at an alternative school for students who had been in the juvenile justice system, many formerly incarcerated and attending school because it was a condition of parole. Encouraged by the results in their classroom, Susan shared the way they had built interest-based inquiry units with the curriculum director in the district which gradually spread to other schools. A collaboration with the local teaching college led to the development of new courses on project-based learning for beginning teachers, and later Susan developed an online course to help district teachers build their own units. And it all started with observing students at lunchtime.

## Students in the Driver's Seat

Susan and Vickie knew they weren't reaching their students. It took some careful observation, during a break from the more formal "school time" to notice a subject that mattered to the teens. They had the wisdom to stop and reflect and shift their focus. They decided that, if they were reaching their goals (teaching their students to evaluate texts, write arguments, and support their claims with evidence), they could shift the topic to something more relevant to their students.

Maria Montessori urged preschool teachers to observe children to assess their skills, interests, and readiness. This careful observation does not need to stop at high school, college, or in adult education. In the field of education, interest in connecting learning to students' interests and passions, not just to engage them but to make schooling more relevant to students' lived lives, is increasing. Educators are also interested in helping students develop the mindsets and skills to self-regulate and manage their own learning.

Some might call this "student agency." Agency is a popular term in educational psychology, but with several different meanings and definitions. In the context of designing student-centered learning environments, **student agency** includes:

- student **choice** of learning topics
- centering **student voice** in the classroom through student-centered discourse
- involving students in identifying topics that are **meaningful and relevant** to them
- student **ownership** of the learning process
- students **setting their own goals**, reflecting on these goals, and taking action in their learning to meet them

The dreaded question, "Why do we have to know this?" would never be asked if students had more agency—more choice, voice, and ownership—over their own learning. Ultimately agency is about sparking motivation, which Daniel Pink, in his book *Drive* (2011), suggests has three components: autonomy, mastery, and purpose. When students experience lessons that give them freedom and ownership, and have an opportunity to master skills, it puts them in the driver's seat of their education. Then "student engagement" is no longer a problem.

Research has demonstrated that students who have agency in their learning are more motivated, better at self-regulating their learning, more resilient, and—as a result—are more likely to achieve academic success (Lin-Siegler et al. 2016; Pintrich 2003).

Student agency expert, author, and researcher Nancy Gerzon asks us not to stop at who chooses the topics, but to take a close look at who is setting the learning goals in the classroom. Teachers often feel tied to externally developed goals (pacing guides, district mandates or testing dates, for example). But we can share the goal setting process with our students in the classroom in many ways.

Nancy explains the importance of shared goal setting:

> The single most important thing is that students co-construct what it will look like when they're successful as part of the process of every lesson. That internalization by students of what the learning will look like changes the zone of proximal development. It also changes equity factors in the room. Giving students who need more support and understanding is not magical. [Collaborative goal setting] helps them to see what *success looks like.*

## The Power of a Checklist

Shifting agency in the classroom toward students can be as simple as creating a student checklist. During the first months of the 2020 pandemic, the students in Jess Gribbon's eighth grade class were on a rotating schedule, one week "on" in the classroom, then two weeks off at home. Not surprisingly, many were falling behind in their work. At home, many other distractions and family responsibilities arose, including work and younger siblings to take care of. Who would have the time to read *A Midsummer Night's Dream*?

Jess started from a place of curiosity. She noticed some students had multiple assignments with zeros, and she wanted to understand what was getting in the way for those kids. She wanted to figure out a way for her students to share with her what their barriers were and to empower them to address their challenges, particularly when they were not in school.

She devised a checklist—a simple Google form for students to complete once a week so they could reflect on their satisfaction with their work. For each assignment, students would check green (I turned it in, and I'm satisfied with my grade), yellow (I turned it in, but I would like to make revisions or get feedback on my work), or red (I turned it in, but it's incomplete). She saw quick results: "I had eight who were failing and who were on my watch list—who I need to keep an eye out for. And *all eight of them* ended up passing with this checklist." All eight students used the new system to get caught up with their work and to ask for help when they needed it.

When students returned to a full-time schedule, Jess added one extra step: She held a Friday morning workshop for students who had missing or incomplete assignments and needed more support. Students who had completed their assignments to their own satisfaction had the time to work on other assignments or go to the library, which also incentivized them to manage their time and keep on top of their work. In her redesign of the students' weekly activities, Jess shifted from a focus on accountability and grades to supporting students to reflect on and keep track of their progress. Students could now rethink, redo and resubmit their work, focusing on improvement, which shifted the agency from the teacher to the students.

Jess reports that the students also learned important life skills as a side benefit: "I feel like this is setting them up to be successful. Because they have practiced managing their time, prioritizing assignments, understanding deadlines, and feeling comfortable and confident in asking for extra help, instead of just silently struggling."

Sofi Frankowski, chief learning officer at Schools That Lead, the improvement network that was supporting Jess, sums up the power of this simple shift in practice:

> If you have an eighth grader who leaves eighth grade with an F in English and goes to high school, that kid is not set up for success. That kid does not start high school from a positive place. If we can help them see themselves as learners and as kids who belong at school and have something to give and ideas worthy of having and sharing, then I think we've *really changed* a kid's trajectory.

Sofi describes the shift as freedom: "I think it is first the freedom from being judged. Then it's freedom from judging themselves. And then it just becomes flexibility and learning—and trying and learning some more. And isn't that what we want for our kids and our grown-ups?"

Jess's checklist was more than a quick and clever way of keeping track of students' assignments. It was an invitation to students to have agency and control over their own learning process and communicated an open door, conveying *I'm here to help you on your learning journey.*

## Talk Less, Smile More

When my colleague Peter Brunn, vice president of organizational learning at the Center for the Collaborative Classroom, observes classrooms, he asks a simple question: "Who is doing most of the work?" One way to answer this question is to look at who is doing most of the talking in the room.

Peter was collaborating with our team at the Regional Educational Laboratory West at WestEd in Reno, Nevada. We were coaching teams of teachers in two schools over three years, supporting them as they focused on K–6 writing instruction and made incremental improvements to their practice. They were learning to teach a new curriculum called *Being a Writer,* so it was an ideal time to reflect on instructional practice. We started with the question: How much time do students get to write during each lesson? Research suggests that students write every day, but we knew from prior implementations of the curriculum that establishing consistent writing time for students would represent a challenging shift for the teachers (Graham et al 2012).

Teachers in Caree Walker's first grade team tracked their lesson time for two weeks, some with elaborate spreadsheets, others with notes on the back of a piece of paper. According to the curriculum, the ideal amount of writing time was between ten and twenty minutes, depending on the students' grade level. Caree and her co-teacher aimed for fifteen minutes a day of writing. Having two teachers in the classroom made the data collection even easier, as one could be the official timer. They timed the first part of the lesson, which was teacher-led, and also timed the second part of the lesson, when students were writing in their writers' notebooks. What they found surprised them. Some days they were approaching ten minutes. Other days, they simply ran out of time. The teacher-directed part of the lesson was completely taking over the essential time for students to practice writing.

Part of our role was to support the teachers in developing "change ideas" to test in their classrooms. A change idea is a term used in the improvement science community to describe an alteration to a practice that interrupts how work is usually done. The change idea is implemented in an improvement cycle (or a plan-do-study-act cycle) to test a theory (e.g., if I try x, then y might happen). Ideally, change ideas are small, attainable, high-impact and low-effort shifts in practice that occur on a regular (daily or weekly) basis. Caree's change idea was to preplan her lesson with her main talking points so that she didn't infringe on her students' writing time at the end of the lesson. The shift was tiny, but it produced an important result. Over time students began to write up to twenty minutes a day—more than twice the amount of time students had spent writing before Caree took a close look at her teaching. Not surprisingly, the students' writing also improved in quantity and quality.

This was where I saw the power of the small shift in teaching. Caree's motivation was to increase her students' writing time. She had a concrete goal. Then she became aware of where her behaviors were getting in the way of that goal: She was talking too much. With the small additional step of planning to just teach the most important parts of the lesson, she was able to increase the time her students had for independent work. It was only a matter of minutes, but over weeks and months this translated into many more hours of writing time for her students. And there was an added benefit: During this independent writing time, Caree was able to build in more peer-to-peer feedback and teacher-student writing conferences. (More on how educators can support small shifts in Chapter 6: Teachers at the Center.)

It turns out that supporting student agency can be as simple as shifting who is doing most of the talking.

## A Culture of Trust

In the 1990s, I spent a year in a journalism program studying Esther Wojcicki, the lead teacher and advisor, for my doctoral dissertation (Austin 2000). Her program was well known for creating high-quality, award-winning newspapers and had grown in popularity in the school over the years. Beyond these accolades, Esther herself was becoming known in the community, not just for her teaching, but for her writing and parenting. She is sometimes referred to as the "godmother of Silicon Valley" as one of her daughters became the CEO of 23andMe, another became the CEO of YouTube, and another is a professor of pediatric medicine. She has a strong parenting philosophy (see her book, *How to Raise Successful People*) that parallels her teaching philosophy (see *Moonshots in Education*). The notion of supporting children and students to make their own choices and pursue them with independence—and trusting them to lead—is core to her approach. Trust is the first ingredient in her recipe for success:

> The first thing to establish in the classroom is a culture of trust. That does not mean that students are given complete freedom to run wild and do what they want. It means the students trust each other to help in the learning process, and the teacher trusts the students. Since the teacher is in control, he or she must take the initiative. Teachers need to put themselves into situations that require students to be trustworthy.

In her books, she introduces the acronym she created to help people understand what she does in her classroom to empower students: trust, respect, independence, collaboration, and kindness (TRICK). She believes these are the most important attributes of a classroom culture that empowers students. The teacher needs to create a culture where the students feel respected and where they are given as much independence as possible. If a student makes a mistake, they can expect to be treated with kindness and understanding.

I spent my time in Esther's classrooms trying to understand how she was able to support her students to become so independent in their learning. I discovered that Esther provides student agency in every way: Students in her beginning and advanced journalism classes can *choose* the topics they are writing about, so they are personally *meaningful and relevant*, and she engages them in *discussions* about politics, current events, and the attributes of high-quality writing. Ultimately, she lays the foundation for the students to *own the process* and *reflect on their learning* by evaluating each newspaper as it comes out and considering what they can improve on in the next issue. They also engage with clear models for what counts as high quality writing. By the end of their time in the program in advanced journalism, the teacher is barely visible. It seems like the students are running the program. However, even when the student editors become the teachers, Esther is still very involved, as she explains:

> I'm watching what's going on in class. Although everybody else is in charge, it's like a tennis game for me. I'm watching this ball, and when I find that it doesn't land where it's supposed to land, then I do a correction. Sometimes I have to say nothing, and sometimes I have to do a correction after hours, but I've got to watch what's going on or lose touch with the whole program. Like right now, they're doing a men's issues page. I said, "Men's issues? Men's issues? I mean, the whole world is called 'his-tory!'"

Encouraging students' agency doesn't mean giving up all control of the classroom, rather designing a learning environment that provides opportunities for students to be in charge and take an active role in their learning (as I discuss in the next chapter on active learning).

When teachers provide opportunities for students to choose topics that are meaningful and relevant to them, support them to reflect on their own goals and progress, and give them enough time to practice what they learn, they become accountable for their own learning. But a student-centered approach takes courage to step back and give students the time and space to try, to practice what they learn, to fail, and to try again. After all, at its core, isn't that what learning is all about?

### Reflecting on Student Agency

To sum up, Susan and Vickie made a powerful shift in their teaching when they recognized that focusing on content that resonated with their students would lead to more engagement. Jess implemented a new tool for students to monitor their own learning and provided the opportunity to retry assignments until they were satisfied. Caree took a close look at the discourse patterns in her room and adjusted, and Esther established learning environments where her students could become leaders and teachers.

How can we begin to reflect on our own practice of supporting student agency? If you are a leader who works with teachers, you might have teachers read this chapter and reflect on their current practice, scaffolded by the reflection questions below. If you are a teacher, you might use the questions to reflect on your teaching, discuss one question with your colleagues in your professional learning community (PLC) or consider one small shift to make this week or this month.

## Reflection Questions: Agency
- Who is involved in choosing the topics of study?
- Who sets the learning goals and evaluates progress toward those goals?
- Who is doing most of the talking in the room?
- Who is doing most of the work in the learning activities?
- Who gets the opportunity to lead the learning?

## CHAPTER 2

# Learn by Doing

*If we taught babies to talk as most skills are taught in school,
they would memorize lists of sounds in a predetermined order
and practice them alone in a closet.*

—LINDA DARLING-HAMMOND

I sat on the floor of a darkened room, peering through a small opening in a black curtain. Through the opening, I could observe a mother sitting in a chair with a baby in her lap. The baby listened to a pre-recorded sentence and then turned her gaze to one of two television screens with cartoon characters. This was my job on Tuesday afternoons in high school. Why was I there? To watch carefully and press on the right or left clickers in my hand to capture which direction the baby was looking.

Believe it or not, the direction of the baby's gaze could tell us if they understood the concept of transitive verbs (that is, verbs that are used with an object). If the baby looked to the correct side, they hypothesized that she understood what was being said by the actions of the character on the screen. The researchers had identified a tiny window into the infants' preverbal brain. How does a baby learn grammar? Certainly not through a lecture. An infant learns about language through experiences with a more expert language user. Interacting, participating, experiencing, and engaging in trial and error—this is how we naturally learn. Why aren't more schools set up for interaction, authentic experiences, and safe and supportive spaces for these activities?

## Math as an Activity

We happened upon thirty-five such supportive spaces when we surveyed some teachers. One fall, in the heart of the COVID-19 pandemic, my colleagues at the Regional Educational Laboratory West and ULEAD (Utah Leading Through Effective, Actionable, and Dynamic Education) gathered a group of elementary math teachers on Zoom. They had been identified as "bright spot" teachers in the state of Utah based on the gains their students had made on math tests. We knew from student achievement data that fifth and eighth grade math scores were dropping precipitously throughout the state. We were curious, what were these teachers doing that led to such standout results in their classrooms? In advance of the convening, we suggested that teachers post a bright spot from their classrooms on a Padlet bulletin board.

One teacher posted:

A recent bright spot in my mathematics teaching is watching students collaborate and communicate in order to complete tasks. Students collaborated with each other on how to enlarge a 2D dragon to become a mural, six times as big as the original! They began with a one-by-one inch square and transferred the lines and shapes to make a mural. They did not know what they were drawing! When they worked to piece it together, they were amazed.

A sixth-grade teacher posted:

So many students come into class being able to do an algorithm without deeper understanding. Teaching students that each problem can tell a story and have a visual representation, can be written about, and can be expressed with an equation or expression is powerful for them.

A third wrote:

> One of the bright spots in my math teaching is when my students feel confident enough to start teaching their peers. Creating a safe environment where kids take risks and feel it's ok to make mistakes plays a very important role in creating these beautiful moments.

What struck me from their comments was how the teachers in our convening were singularly focused on math as an activity: that is, learning through collaboration, visualizing complex concepts, and doing hands-on work. They didn't see their job as being the smartest one in the room, but designing experiences where students were actively engaged with math.

This included art, movement, and other modes of learning beyond sitting and listening or what Harvard psychologist Howard Gardner calls "multiple intelligences"—that is, the variety of ways humans process information. His original six intelligences were: linguistic, musical, logical-mathematical, spatial-visual, bodily-kinesthetic, intra and interpersonal (Gardner 1985). Putting together a mural of a dragon involves physically moving to create a piece, using visual and spatial skills to place the pieces, and using logic and critical thinking. And if you are doing it in a group, those interpersonal skills are also needed.

A lot of attention in the education community is currently focused on "student engagement," in part because the COVID-19 pandemic forced so many schools and districts into distance learning. We lost a lot of student engagement—even just plain student attendance—along the way. These standout Utah teachers were focused not just on engaging students but on creating activities that invited students to participate in different ways: physically, socially, and cognitively.

## Becoming Mathematicians

Authors Jal Mehta and Sarah Fine went searching for bright spots in their book *In Search of Deeper Learning* (2019). They also landed on this idea of math as an activity as they studied math teaching at Bryant High School, a school that serves high poverty students of color in a major northeastern city. They noticed this sentence posted on the wall of one classroom: "Math is an activity: questioning, noticing, calculating, exploring, organizing, persevering, making sense, understanding, applying connections" (Mehta and Fine 2019, 320).

Two classrooms, taught by Nathaniel Martin and Nick Collins, stood out. Their students played math games and solved math problems but in a very hands-on way. In one class, students blew up balloons to determine the relationship between the balloon's circumference and the number of breaths, and in another, students developed strategies while playing a game that involved crossing out lines and dots.

Martin, a first-year teacher, describes his goal: "Our purpose is not to get them into college; our purpose is to give students power. The idea is to help students become mathematicians, which means they have to do what real mathematicians do—discover, innovate, and meet a real intellectual need" (2019, 324).

Collins, Martin's experienced co-teacher, describes his role in shaping the learning environment: "My underlying philosophy is that math and mathematically thinking and solving puzzles is something which is innately enjoyable. It's not so much that I have to convince them; it's more that I have to *remove the reasons* that it's not coming to life for them" (2019, 325, emphasis added). His message to his students is that math is not something you receive, it's something you do. For these teachers, it is a matter of redesigning classes in a way that gives students more agency and opportunities for active learning.

As Mehta and Fine sum up:

> [The teachers] had not found some magical way to make mathematics more engaging. They had simply, and significantly, *changed the tasks* asked of students— play mathematical games, reason collectively about puzzling mathematical conundrums—and through these processes they were gradually teaching topics like discrete mathematics and statistical analysis (2019, 326, emphasis added).

## Hands-On, Minds-On, and Collaborative

The field of education has seen waves of interest in active learning—whether it was "progressive education" in John Dewey's time, "discovery learning" in the seventies and eighties, or project-based learning more recently. These labels have both helped and hindered a shift toward more active learning in the classroom. They have provided "visions of the possible," but have also been intimidating. Such classrooms can require a complete upheaval of business-as-usual, in systems that traditionally have not supported teaching that is more student-centered. However, if we can consider the different ways students can be invited to become more active in their learning, we can make small shifts toward more student-centered learning environments.

Active learning is not a new concept. Education powerhouses Dewey, Vygotsky, and Piaget all put forth theories that learning happens through specific kinds of interactions with more expert others. They all challenged the notion of students as passive learners or empty vessels to be filled. Instead, they argued that the teacher's role is to create learning environments to challenge students so that they can construct their own knowledge. The teacher must also guide them as they engage in activities.

As we design **active learning** tasks for students we can consider:

- the **purpose** of the activity—not just the "what" but the "why" behind it
- **social interaction** and opportunities for student-to-student collaboration
- **"minds-on" cognitive tasks** and challenging, real-life problems to solve

- **"hands-on" and physically active** tasks through art, engineering, design, technology, dance, drama and movement
- multiple intelligences, multiple representations, and **rich contexts for learning**

A report from the National Comprehensive Center for Teacher Quality includes active learning experiences as a key element of high-quality teaching and cites research on the positive impact of interactive teaching practices on students' achievement in mathematics at all grade levels and in elementary reading, in particular (Goe and Stickler 2008). They also note that the quality of teachers' assignments is positively associated with elementary math and secondary reading achievement.

In his article, "Possible Futures: Toward a New Grammar of Schooling" (2022), Jal Mehta describes the importance of purposeful learning activities:

> If the future of pre-K–12 education is going to be significantly better than the past, then we need to replace this entrenched grammar of schooling with an approach that values teaching and learning more than control, liberation more than colonization, sustainable approaches more than quick fixes, and human relationships more than bureaucratic rules... We need a different social contract grounded in the idea that children are *curious, capable, interested people*, whose personhood needs to be respected and whose interests can be stimulated. Such a contract must start with giving students a *clear purpose* for their learning,

moving from *what* they are learning to *why*. Purposes come in many shapes, and developing one is a critical starting point for any journey of consequential learning (Mehta 2022, emphases added).

We know that active learning with a purpose within a culture of collaboration helps students to develop social and emotional skills, perform better academically, and enhances their sense of belonging in the classroom (Barron & Darling-Hammond, 2008; Cantor et al 2029; Darling-Hammond et al., 2019). Active learning experiences are key to student engagement and opportunities to learn. Even though humans are inherently social, students need to build collaboration skills throughout their lives. And the more connected students feel to school the more effort they will put into learning.

In their review of research of inquiry-based and cooperative learning Stanford professors Brigid Barron and Linda Darling-Hammond cite multiple studies comparing traditional versus inquiry-based approaches to teaching (Barron & Darling-Hammond 2008). These studies provide evidence of the positive impact of hands-on, minds-on opportunities to learn, including: improved critical thinking skills, problem solving ability, attitude toward learning, increased confidence in learning, and equal or better performance on standardized tests. An impressive list! They sum up their findings: "A growing body of research has shown... Active learning practices have a more significant impact on student performance than *any other variable*, including student background and prior achievement" (Barron and Darling-Hammond 2008, 8, emphases added).

The reason my eighth-grade field trip to the forest, prairie, and desert of Washington State was so memorable (aside from the opportunity to gossip about boys in our tents at night) was because the purpose was clear. We were doing a comparative study of the soil and water of the region. We were actively engaged, acting as environmental scientists, as we collected our soil and water samples. The process was collaborative: One held the string while another staked the plot and a third held the clipboard and took notes. And most important, it was in the real world. We had done significant preparation in the classroom, but we were also able to extend our learning beyond the classroom walls.

## English Inc.

These real-world connections can be made across subjects and grade levels. Consider a group of teachers in an East Bay Area high school who were teaching a traditional British literature–focused English class. They couldn't understand why their students weren't as excited about the novels as they were. The team recognized that something needed to change. With some funding from their principal, they completely revamped their twelfth grade English curriculum and transformed their course, but with small shifts.

The teachers began by interviewing professors at their local community college, as well as some industry professionals. They asked them: What workforce readiness skills do you want to see in your incoming students and prospective employees?

My colleague, Pam Fong, senior research associate at WestEd—who was part of the teaching team—recounted to me what they learned, with some excitement:

> It came down to four things: an ability to collaborate with different personalities and different working styles, an ability to communicate verbally and in writing, critical thinking skills, and, finally, accountability, so that students follow through and are responsible for their actions.

They took their traditional English class and redesigned it based on these four pillars. Pam paused as she thought back to that time as a new teacher, "Once we had it in place, we knew this was going to be a huge leap for the students. Nothing like this had ever been expected of them."

The first semester they started with a small change: putting their students in groups to discuss a novel, instead of discussing it as a whole class. Pam noticed a change right away:

> One of the things I realized was instead of feeling like I had to teach thirty-two students, I was only teaching eight groups. The kids had a layer of support by being in these groups. I wasn't always aware of every challenge that they encountered because their peers

helped to resolve them. I spent my time in classes walking from group to group and checking in and supporting their problem solving.

Pam and her team intentionally built in a lot of scaffolding for their students to learn how to work together and speak respectfully to each other. This included role playing different scenarios and helping students to reflect on what kinds of behavior supported discussions and what moves could shut it down. Many students, particularly the higher performing ones, noticed that it was much harder to work collaboratively than alone. As they practiced taking on different roles in their groups, they also observed their classmates' contributions. They noticed who displayed the skills that would support or hinder their work and which personalities they meshed well with. This information was important when it came time to choose their team for their final group project.

By the end of the year, the students were in consistent teams, had developed a company name and a logo for their team, and each had specific roles. The teachers had based the project on an approach to group work founded by Stanford University professors Elizabeth Cohen and Rachel Lotan (Cohen and Lotan 2014). In a culminating activity, students became business consultants and were presented with a case study about a fast-food company that was in trouble. They had to research solutions and then develop written and oral arguments which were formally presented to a small restaurant owner in the community.

The teachers also added an element of competition. Only one winning proposal would be chosen by the restaurant owner, which motivated the teams to try to out-do their peers. Pam recalls, "Students within their company teams were valued for contributing strengths such as leadership, organization, creativity, and problem-solving. The success of any team doing well on their projects genuinely required the work of each team member, as the projects depended upon the efforts of multiple people and their roles."

One particular moment that year stood out for Pam:

> I was just sitting on my stool listening to the activity in the room. And I was thinking, "Gosh, I'm so proud of these guys. They really came a long way where they're actually engaged in the text and working together." It was a neat shift, just having that moment. I remember that I didn't feel like an English teacher, but rather a coach helping them learn and master life skills, which we then expected them to demonstrate in their projects. It made teaching so much more interesting and fun. And I wasn't as exhausted.

The teachers' practice had shifted over time from introducing a text, reviewing literary devices, and having a whole class discussion—where only a quarter of the students would contribute—to small groups analyzing texts, working in teams, practicing communication skills, while engaging in a real-world scenario with real-life stakes.

## Small Shifts Toward Active Learning

In real life, learning seldom happens as we passively listen. Sure, we will occasionally listen to a speech, watch a TED Talk, or take in a presidential debate. And there is a place in education for a really good lecture or story (like the ones in this book). However, most of our work and life outside of school is full of interactions—interactions with other people, wrestling with tricky problems, and engaging with the world around us. Redesigning classes to become student-centered involves fundamentally changing the nature of traditional school activity—from passive to active. This means shifting what goes on in the classroom so that students have the power to discover, to innovate, to struggle, and to create. When teachers take a risk and step back from being at the center of the activity, it can make the educational experience more joyful not just for students, but for teachers too.

Remember our journalism teacher, Esther Wojcicki—or "Woj," as her students call her? She shared with me the key to creating more active learning environments and the importance of shifting ownership from the teacher to the students:

> There were times when I first started that I didn't want to continue, just because it's much harder to teach somebody to do something well than to do it yourself. I mean I could do the whole paper myself in less time than it takes them to do all this stuff. And then I realized it wasn't the accomplishing it that was important. It was the process. They learn from the process, and so I should just cool it, relax, and

not worry about it. So, I changed the ownership from myself to them, and it was their paper, their project, their everything, and I would become the consultant, the advisor, the teacher.

Some teachers might be wary that moving toward active learning means they must sacrifice content or feel that they have to wait until testing is over to do the "fun stuff." As we will see in the next chapter, building content knowledge on a base of student activity is possible. Because ultimately, isn't it more tiring to do the work ourselves, as Esther says, than to make the time and space for our *students* to do the work of learning?

## Reflection Questions: Active Learning

Here are some questions for reflection focused on active learning. If you are a leader who works with teachers, you might read the chapter together and reflect on current practice. If you are a teacher, you might use the questions to reflect on your current practice or choose one small shift to focus on this week or this month.

- What is the purpose of the task, lesson, or unit?
- How well does the task, lesson, or unit purpose align to learning goals for students?
- How can students be invited to engage socially and collaborate with each other?
- What are some authentic and engaging "minds-on" problems students can tackle that require them to transfer their learning from one situation to another?

- How can the learning experience involve "hands on" activities in visual arts, drama, dance or movement, engineering, design, or technology?

# CHAPTER 3

# Pass the Mic

*Intelligent novices are those who, although they may not possess the background knowledge needed in a new field, know how to go about gaining that knowledge.*

—ANN BROWN AND JOE CAMPIONE

In 1993, I spent a summer contemplating the disappearance of the golden toad of Monteverde. I was just out of grad school, my head filled with idealistic visions of student-centered learning, sociocultural theories, and "zones of proximal development." I was lucky enough to land my first real job with the late psychologist Ann Brown and her husband Joe Campione at UC Berkeley as a research assistant. Ann had developed a model of instruction that incorporated many of the major theories in the psychology of learning I had been learning about. It was called "Fostering a Community of Learners." The key curricular elements of this model included small group reading, students doing research on science topics, and a collaborative way of sharing learning (also known as the jigsaw method) (Aronson and Patnoe 1997).

And the toad? We were designing a performance assessment to evaluate what fifth graders had learned from a unit on animal habitats and defense mechanisms. The golden toad of Monteverde—once quite abundant in a small region of Costa Rica—had disappeared in 1990, and no one was certain why. Our performance assessment presented a few theories for the students to read about and wrestle with to try to determine what had caused the species to become extinct. Was it climate change? Disease? Habitat loss?

In the Fostering a Community of Learners model, students read together in small groups, researched a topic, and presented what they had learned about animals in order to then build upon and expand *each other's* content knowledge (Brown 1997). But in reality, the magic ingredient underlying all this work was the cultivation of curiosity. Educators came from far and wide to study what students in these Oakland, California schools were doing: digging deep into content, reading sophisticated texts, and teaching each other what they had learned—like mini-professors.

## Baby Steps

Six years later, a group at Stanford University—led by my advisor, educational psychologist Lee Shulman and his wife, Judy Shulman—received a grant to try to replicate what Ann and Joe had developed. We had seen amazing results in two elementary "beta" schools—young students having sophisticated discussions and truly becoming experts in biological science.

Our research group fanned out to elementary, middle, and high schools in the Bay Area where we were trying to create the same conditions, but in many ways we failed. Most of the classrooms where we were working did not end up looking like the sophisticated beehive of productive activity we had observed in the original sites.

The sixth-grade math and science teacher I was coaching provided some clues as to why. Natalie Gale was an energetic, athletic teacher—and a daily swimmer—who loved to share stories and bounce around the room. She literally held the students' attention much of the day with the force of her personality. But she was extremely nervous about sending her kids off to groups to work without her.

She shared her fears privately with me and admitted, "There's a lot more room for things to become chaotic."

My job was to coach her toward more student-centered practice. We started with shifting student discourse, the foundation of any classroom. First, we practiced student-to-student talk with the whole class. One day we sat in a large circle, and Natalie posed questions about the reading on the structure of cells while the students tossed a "talking ball" around the room to each other. The next day the students passed a ball of yarn to each person who spoke, which created a spider-webbed visual of the patterns of student talk in the class. We were gradually shifting the authority from the teacher (and "teacher knows all") to the students ("we can become experts together"). By the time we moved to small groups, Natalie was more comfortable with the busy buzz of the classroom, and her role of bouncing around the front of the room shifted to bouncing from table to table.

At the end of the project, she said to me, "I really need to remember that if I do let go of some of that control, things do happen. That's a huge thing for the teacher. If your expectations are high enough and you teach them how to do something, they will do it, but they're not going to do it if you don't let them." The spark for her was when she saw what her students could accomplish in their small research groups *without* her.

It took giving up her practice of being the authority—and the primary content expert—in the room and letting go of being in charge. For Natalie, it wasn't a just matter of implementing a new curriculum, or introducing group structures, it was changing her mindset about what a teacher does and what her role was in her classroom. Incremental shifts, from teaching at the front of the room, to sitting in a circle, to facilitating small groups, helped her to see her teaching in a new way. At the end of the year, Natalie reflected on how independent her groups had become, when she said, "If I'd wanted to go sit at my desk, I could have."

In her exit interview she reflected to me:

> They can do this if they're taught how to do it and if the expectations are high enough. There were a lot of times when we got into our final groups where I would be amazed. They were really monitoring each other's behavior. They were really taking responsibility for getting things done. There was a big pride and a big self-esteem boost. And I knew they were doing it because of what *I'd been doing.*

### Distributing Expertise

When we introduce projects and active learning, and shift toward student agency, we sometimes worry about "coverage." Will the students learn what we need them to learn? If we spend so much time learning something in depth, then won't we "lose" time on other topics? But I would argue that focusing on a topic in depth not only engages students and impacts motivation, but also provides opportunities to practice those essential skills for becoming an expert on *anything.* Skills like asking good questions, building a foundation of literacy skills, knowing how to conduct research and evaluate sources, and presenting what you learn to an audience. (I delve more into the topic of authentic audiences in the next chapter.) And it's even better if the content areas and disciplines we typically think of as separate (English, social studies, etc.) are integrated and have an opportunity to inform each other, as they do in contexts outside of school.

In the nineties, when we were doing this work, there was a lot of interest in "distributed expertise" and creating classrooms that mirror how we learn in the real world in communities of practice (Brown et al 1997). Distributing expertise across the ecosystem of the classroom fosters independence and provides opportunities for learning and skill-building that support depth over breadth. Some would call this the ideal classroom setting for a "constructivist model" of teaching and learning. In the 2020s, this school of thought connects to "deeper learning" initiatives, project-based learning, and twenty-first century skills (particularly collaboration, communication, and critical thinking). And underlying all these approaches is the importance of developing social skills for collaborative learning.

Several key ideas are nested in the concept of distributing expertise. Distributing expertise in the classroom and developing **student authority** mean:

- recognizing classrooms as **social arenas** or communities of learners engaged in rich content learning

- providing **structures of work**—like group work—that recognize students as developing experts
- giving students responsibility for **sharing their learning** (in effect, the students become teachers)
- creating an **atmosphere of mutual dependency** and trust on a foundation of talk
- supporting the **development of skills and knowledge** in the process of becoming experts, not in isolation (that is, reading, writing, researching, and critical thinking are intertwined and purposeful)

This is the ideal. In reality, tension exists between the teacher being the ultimate authority and students becoming authorities on a topic. However, if we don't recognize students' agency and the importance of active learning, we are ignoring how people naturally learn—through rich engagement with each other and with content. The development of expertise should be one of the primary goals of schooling. This is key to my framework of student-centered learning as it answers the question: What are students becoming knowledgeable about? And what are the mechanisms by which they learn?

In 2000, the National Research Council published a large summary of research on learning called *How People Learn.* A key body of research cited is how novices become experts in a field, whether it's becoming an expert in chess or in physics. Researchers found that becoming an expert does not simply involve acquiring facts and strategies but having an opportunity to learn with understanding, develop conceptual frameworks, and use that knowledge flexibly.

Experts also know how to use metacognitive strategies. That is, they know how to monitor what they know and what they don't know. Teaching students metacognitive strategies has been shown to improve understanding in physics, writing, math, and reading (National Research Council 2000). A recent large-scale analysis of over 2500 studies found that supporting students to use metacognitive strategies and reflect on their learning is one of the most impactful instructional strategies, particularly for elementary-aged students and across grade levels in math and science (Education Endowment Foundation 2021). Integrate metacognition, collaboration (another high-impact, evidence-based instructional strategy), and students solving problems together and building on each other's knowledge, and you have a powerful combination.

The implication for teaching is that our K–12 learning environments need to provide students opportunities to deeply learn content, reflect on and monitor their own learning, and develop independence while learning together. As we will learn in our next story, community-based projects are great settings for supporting students in becoming experts in charge of their learning.

## Second Grade Citizen Activists

Sometimes just taking a moment to step out of the classroom can change the dynamic of who is the authority in the room. Aaron Phillips, second grade teacher at Grayson Elementary, began his unit on civics and government with a trip to the playground. But this trip wasn't for swinging on the monkey bars. Armed with notebooks and pencils, each of his second graders scoured the play-ground like detectives with magnifying glasses. Their job was to look for things their city government could fix, whether it was adding more bark under the swings, or removing an old pipe sticking out of the ground. Aaron describes the scene at the park: "All the kids were engaged and all the kids were interested. That is when they can shine, and you can see a total difference in the learning."

Back in the classroom, Aaron helped the students do online research to determine which departments in their local government might be able to make the changes they wanted. Fast forward a few weeks, and the children welcomed their City Councilman Randy Carter to the classroom with a handshake at the door. He took his seat in one of the small chairs at the front of the audience, near some of the children's parents. Each second grader had their moment to speak. One by one, they climbed up on a box so that they could see—just barely—over the top of the adult-sized podium. Each one took the microphone and made their case while pointing to photos of the playground and the swings projected on a nearby screen. The photographs in their slide deck were labeled with words or phrases like "messy" and "hard ground."

At the end of the presentation, City Councilman Carter stood up to speak and promised to make the improvements the children had suggested. He said, with a pleased smile, "They were able to show me with pictures and data exactly what the problems are, and I will act on their proposal immediately."

Dark-haired Corina summed up her experience with a one-shoulder shrug: "It just makes myself proud that I'm helping the whole community."

Some things to notice from this example: the students were becoming the experts on their dilapidated playground (becoming researchers) and how their city government worked (developing content knowledge). They had the opportunity to present their newfound knowledge in a public presentation (practicing oral language, written language, and presentation skills). They had a real purpose and a real audience. They were also given real-world responsibility to make their case to their city councilman. Their teacher was the facilitator. He organized the field trip, he helped the students learn about the different branches of government, and he supported them to write and practice their speeches. Not to mention, the kids had a real stake in the outcome—an improved playground for their community.

Researchers at the University of Michigan shared Mr. Phillip's story as an example of Project PLACE or "Project-Approach to Literacy and Civic Engagement." They studied forty-eight classrooms in twenty elementary schools and discovered that, in high poverty communities, this kind of project-based learning can produce gains in student social studies and informational reading achievement compared with traditional instruction (Duke et al 2021). Researcher Nell Duke points to the importance of intentional lessons: "In every lesson there's a direct connection between what the students are doing and that ultimate purpose that they have" (Edutopia 2017). Duke's colleague

Anne-lise Halvorsen highlights the importance of student motivation: "Children are curious about the world around them. They're curious about issues in their community and what adults do" (Edutopia 2017). Putting students at the center of their learning experience means centering students' curiosity.

## Who's the Teacher in the Room?

When we bring up the image of "teacher" most of us picture the expert, the authority, a sage, an all-knowing source of information. I continue to be fascinated when I observe preschoolers playing school. It invariably involves one demanding child lording it over a small group of followers. Sometimes with a pointy stick! Unfortunately, this image is a barrier to student-centered learning. If the teacher knows everything, how will the student gain all that knowledge? Students are not empty vessels to be filled. Some of the most profound innovations in education have been attempts to flip that script and invest in the development of student expertise. Unfortunately, this is also one of the hardest shifts for us to make. We need to understand a content area well enough to not "teach it," but to design opportunities for students to play "junior versions" of the whole game. (I explain more on that topic in Chapter 5 on Apprenticeship.) Small shifts in letting go of being the primary authority in the room can make space for this kind of student growth.

I asked Esther, our journalism teacher, how she saw her role in the journalism program. By the time her students had progressed to the advanced program, as juniors and seniors, they were leading their peers and in charge of every aspect of the newspaper, from the business side—securing ads, paying the printer—to the editing of articles, to the distribution of the paper.

Here's how she describes her role:

> Well, I'm like the hub of the whole thing. The kids are in charge. That's exactly what I want. But the funny part is they look like they're in charge, but they aren't totally in charge. But that's my view of the way the program should run. How ridiculous it would be for me to be in charge. What would I be learning? They would be learning the same old routine, which is, teacher in front, students taking instruction. I'm just like the CEO of the company. He's in charge, but he's not putting the nuts and bolts in the thing.

What's even more fun is asking the advanced journalism students what *they* think Esther's role is. Here is a sample of their responses:

> She's like a general overseer who doesn't really lay hands too much down. She knows what's going on.

> She'll offer advice but she won't micromanage.

> She keeps order, but lets us do what we want.

> She supervises us, but usually lets us alone.

She's like the Wizard of Oz, you know, she's like behind the curtain.

Ultimately Esther provides her students a learning experience that mirrors the context of many workplaces—working in collaborative groups, supervised but not micromanaged.

I've noticed that some school districts are replacing the term teacher with "facilitator" of learning, and students are now "learners." If you had to choose a new word or phrase for the teacher's role, designing experiences for students to become experts, what would it be?

## Reflection Questions: Student Authority

Here are some questions for reflection focused on developing student authority. If you are a leader who works with teachers, you might have teachers reflect on their current practice or choose one small shift to make this week or this month. If you are a teacher, you might use the questions to reflect on your current practice or identify one question to discuss with your colleagues.

- How can we support students to become experts? How can we step back as the expert so that students can step forward?
- How do the patterns of talk, the nature of assignments, and the intended audiences for student work reflect who is the authority in the room?

- In what ways can going deeper into content also support students' development of essential academic skills (reading, writing, critical thinking)?
- How can we build in opportunities for metacognition and reflection in learning tasks and lessons?
- What kinds of individual and group learning tasks can support students as they develop their knowledge and authority?

# CHAPTER 4

# Publish to the World

*Every day when I wake up I have an important decision to make. Do I write for my teacher or publish to the world? I prefer to publish to the world.*

—A YOUNG WRITER

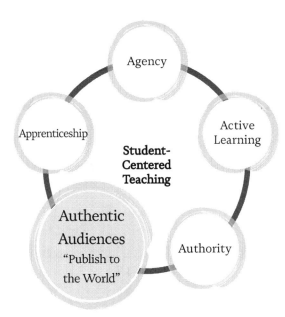

Increasingly young people are finding new audiences for their work, through YouTube channels, TikTok, Instagram, or podcasts. These activities are inherently interesting because they provide choice, ownership, and relevance (agency); they are hands-on and real-world activities (active learning); and they establish the authors as experts in their chosen domains (author-ity). The key ingredient in these activities is an authentic audience. What's sometimes missing—and what a teacher and classmates can provide—is a feedback loop that includes a measure of quality. Although, we certainly have a measure of popularity with all of those clicks and likes!

## Community as Classroom

Every year students in Kai Akana's biology class respond to the question "Are genetically modified organisms inherently good or bad?" His students research and develop arguments for and against GMOs, considering legal, political, social, environmental, and economic perspectives.

One year, Kai wanted to address the disconnect between his students' classroom learning and their lives in their neighborhoods and the larger O'ahu community. He was meeting virtually with a group of teachers who were examining how their students' culture was—or was not—reflected in their curricular programs. Collaborating with other teachers provided him the opportunity to take a step back, examine his curriculum and to culturally attune his genetics unit.

With the support of this teacher group Kai recast his question from "Are GMOs good or bad?" to something more nuanced "Does the GMO papaya contribute to a more just, healthy, and beloved community?" The activity was designed to foster argumentation skills and to explore complicated bioengineering issues from ethical and cultural perspectives. In prior years, students had interviewed politicians, but not their own family members. He felt that shifting the unit to include community members would provide an opportunity for students to learn about multiple perspectives on the topic—to inform their research—as well as provide an opportunity for students to share back what they learned with their community.

His students collected papaya leaf samples in their neighborhoods and genetically sequenced them in their classroom lab. Students also added their geolocated data to an online database and knowledge repository called FieldScope, which helped them to map the locations of the genetically modified, organic, and hybrid papaya trees in their community (Nelson-Barber et al. 2022). Then they took it one step further. They interviewed family members to understand their positions on GMOs.

They asked them, "What is your connection to agriculture and food production?" "What do you know about GMOs?" "How do you feel about GMO crops in our community?" "What are your hopes for food sustainability in our community?"

Students used what they learned from their elders—combined with their findings that 53 percent of the papaya seeds in their neighborhoods were genetically modified—and wrote testimony to advocate their community's positions on GMOs. The final step? Uploading a video of their oral testimony and sharing what they learned with their families.

As Kai reflected to me in an email: "We spend more time in this lesson exploring why family members might feel a certain way, and whether that has to do with generational, political, or cultural influences. It makes the entire lesson much more personal and memorable." Kai was surprised to learn that many of his students disagreed with their elders' point of view about GMOs in their community.

My colleague, Jonathan Boxerman, describes the shift in his NextGenScience blog post, where I first learned about this story: "In revising his unit Mr. Akana deliberately connected ethics rooted in the students' home cultures with family and community perspectives on GMOs. He taught the students how to advocate for the well-being of their community" (Boxerman 2022). Ultimately, he taught his students how to seek out different sources and perspectives for their arguments.

Schooling doesn't happen in a vacuum, although we sometimes pretend that it does. Students and their families bring experiences, points of view, languages, and values to their classrooms. However, too often school assignments ignore the fact that students are people living in communities. When we shift away from assignments with the teacher as the primary audience and toward performances of understanding and public products, we can begin to blur the barriers between schools and the communities where they are located. The teacher shifts from being the grader with the grade book to a designer of tasks with opportunities for feedback from peers and community members. Some have called this "localizing the curriculum." Assignments with authentic audiences provide an opportunity for students to practice real-world activities and receive real feedback on what they are learning.

## High Stakes

Author, educator, and teacher Ron Berger of EL Education is most known for a five-minute video, "Austin's Butterfly." In the video Ron tells a story about first grader Austin who was given the assignment to create a scientific illustration of a tiger swallowtail butterfly. Austin's first draft is not very accurate. It's a simple line drawing without much detail. Ron then coaches a small group of students in the video as they critique Austin's first draft.

He asks them what advice they would give to Austin about the shape of the wings. The students respond: "He could make it pointier." "He could make it more like a triangle shape." As they critique the drawing, Ron shows them how—with the help of his own classmates—Austin's drawing of a butterfly improves from his first draft to his sixth. When Austin's final draft is revealed, students audibly "ooh" as they see how much more accurate

Austin's sixth draft is compared to his first. The video has millions of views and downloads. It's captured the attention of educators because it shows the importance of practice, multiple drafts, critique, and revision.

As Ron explains to me:

> That's a big power of multiple drafts for an authentic audience. It stops being just about pleasing the teacher, and it's about doing it *right for the world*. And that gives a whole different level of motivation. When I went to school, I did work, handed it in and it got marked, and it was given back to me, and I threw it away. It's a very different thing for students to think "We're all going to do five drafts or ten drafts." Because nobody writes a book in one draft. Nobody designs a house in one draft. Nobody does an experiment in one trial. And when you're on a soccer team, you practice. When you're in an orchestra, you practice. When you're in a play, you practice, right? It's not just the final performance. *It's the practices.*

As I caught up on Zoom with Ron—twenty years after he taught this lesson—he revealed something surprising. What was most important about Austin's Butterfly was actually never featured in the video. He explained, "What you don't see in that video is the reason Austin was willing to do six drafts was because it went on a card that was *sold all over Idaho* to preserve butterfly environments. There was a *reason* for him to get it right. It was a contribution."

Ron himself was a teacher for twenty-five years in a small, rural, innovative public school where the students' learning was focused on making their town a better place. They learned their math and literacy "in the service of doing something good." His students tested the local well water to make sure it was safe to drink and collaborated with the local university to do the testing in their labs. They tested homes for radon and discovered that fourteen homes had high levels, which can cause lung cancer. The reports the students produced are still in the town hall and the Board of Health even recently requested them. As Ron says, "There couldn't have been higher stakes."

He admits, however, that this kind of teaching takes more work:

> It does take extra time. You've got to make those connections to local experts. You have to find the local projects that really contribute. You've got to figure out how to do field work with kids that matters. I didn't understand radon stuff. So, I never say to teachers, "This is easier." It's harder, but it's more fulfilling. We're in this work because we want to succeed. We want kids to be alive with passion for learning.

Creating community-based projects like these is not an easy lift. So, what about some small shifts? Ron shares a simple example. He visited a kindergarten where the students were studying their community. They had just come back from a field trip to their local fire station, where each student was paired with a firefighter. Their task? To write a thank you note to the firefighter they met with an illustration. As Ron says, for a fifth grader that's a pretty easy task, but for a kindergartener, still learning their letters or how to write a sentence, this is a big challenge. Ron describes the process to me:

> It wasn't a one-day thing. It was a week-long thing because every day they were doing lessons: letter formation, finger spacing, sentences, capitals, and lowercase. The teacher said, "You know there is a good chance your firefighter will put your letter up on her locker and everyone will see it for the next few years." So the kids were obsessed with getting their letter formation perfect and their punctuation perfect and their capitalization perfect. They did draft after draft, and they critiqued each other's drafts, and they posted their work. The lessons that were happening were the same as the lessons in any kindergarten in America. But it wasn't to please the teacher. It was to contribute to the world. *The purpose* is what made it so different.

The passion and engagement in the kindergarten class that Ron describes is what we all want to see come alive in a classroom. That is, kids putting forth their best effort, learning important life skills, and truly caring about the outcomes. Every kindergartener learns to write letters. It was the small shift of having an audience who you admire and respect that made the difference to these young students.

## Making Learning Public

Stephanie Vollmer's second grade classroom was a bustle of activity as parents and grandparents filled the room for the final publishing celebration. Students proudly showed their families their work and read aloud to them in small groups—except for Don. Don sat with his grandmother, his arms crossed, with a determined and sullen look on his face. He did not want to read. His grandmother whispered encouraging words to him. To no avail. Stephanie hurried over to his table. She offered to read his book for him. Don's grandmother offered to read the book. Don wouldn't budge. It took a little investigating to finally learn why.

Stephanie had been participating in an inquiry-based professional learning community through a partnership between her district and Lead by Learning, a program of the School of Education at Mills College at Northeastern University in Oakland, California. She and her colleagues were conducting empathy interviews—or "learning partnership conversations"—with their students to investigate their learning styles. In these one-on-one conversations, teachers invite their students in as partners to help them answer questions about their experience in class. She shared her story in a Lead by Learning blog post (Vollmer 2019).

When she sat down to chat with Don, he firmly and clearly shared that he didn't like reading his writing out loud because he didn't like people looking at him. Stephanie shares some of the new ideas that came out of her conversation with Don:

He thought of some ways he could successfully share in front of a large group, like covering his face with his journal, covering only his eyes with his journal and exposing his mouth, or memorizing his story to be able to share. He was even open to the idea of sharing his story while standing behind his classmates, so they wouldn't be facing him!

Don finally read his story to a few friends, with his journal over his face.

Not every child will feel comfortable with the standard form of sharing. A small shift in teaching allowed this child to make his learning public. The small shift was supported by a professional learning community that put Stephanie's inquiry at the center of *her* learning about her students (more on this kind of teacher learning in Chapter 6). Taking the time to meet one-on-one with a student and hearing his concerns and point of view allowed Stephanie to personalize Don's learning experience.

## Authentic, Relevant, Real-World

Publishing to the world is easier than it has ever been. Young people have their own blogs and TikTok channels. They carry a video production suite literally in their back pocket in the form of a smartphone. My kids often edit our family road trip videos while sitting in the back seat on the long ride home. They also use social media to draw attention to their work. So many amazing youth dancers are getting visibility for their art through their sixty second posts. They know how to build an audience, market a product, and even evaluate their own website data analytics. Some of these students are years ahead of our schools and classrooms in their experience with drafting, editing, and publishing. Our job is to connect these forms of expression and communication to the content knowledge in their curriculum.

Our job is also to understand students' family contexts, so their learning environments better reflect their lived lives. In the field of education, a focus on creating learning opportunities that reflect students' identities, languages, and communities is increasing. This is variously called culturally responsive, culturally relevant, and culturally sustaining education. The bottom line is that when learning is meaningful, relevant, and reflective of students' cultures, students are more likely to engage with, relate to, and understand new content (Priniski et al. 2018; Gay 2018).

We can think about what makes a learning task authentic and relevant in several ways. Finding and providing **authentic audiences** means that students' work:

- **connects to the world** outside of the classroom
- reflects **subject expert practices** (that is, how journalists, scientists, or politicians do their work, for example)
- is **embedded in students' lives** and communities
- is **culturally relevant** and responsive, and reflects students' cultures and experiences
- offers real opportunities for **feedback, reflection, and revision**

Students want to see themselves reflected in the curriculum, whether it's including culturally relevant literature in an English class, connecting to contemporary music and the arts, or providing an opportunity for choice and pursuing your own particular interests and passions. Research shows, for instance, that framing writing projects around personal interests encourages learners, helps them connect background knowledge to new information, and fosters authenticity of learning (Bruning et al. 2011; Gebre & Polman 2020; Bennett et al. 2007).

Authentic audiences are more than motivating to students, they also provide an opportunity to demonstrate learning through performances of understanding versus traditional tests. In "It's time for curriculum mapping 3.0" (2021) author and researcher Jay McTighe proposes a new conception of curriculum, one that focuses on audiences for student learning. He writes:

> Rather than asking, "What will we teach in the curriculum?" (indicating a focus on content inputs), the fundamental curriculum question becomes, *"What should students be able to do with their learning?"* (indicating a focus on student performance). In other words, what if we structured (i.e., mapped) the curriculum around authentic tasks and projects? Authentic tasks call for students to apply (transfer) their learning within a realistic and relevant context. Such tasks include a clear purpose, a target audience, and genuine constraints (e.g., schedule, budget, word count). Since these tasks are typically open ended, they frequently

offer opportunities for students to work toward their strengths and be creative.

Research comparing project-based learning to traditional approaches shows that project-based learning units not only require critical thinking skills, knowledge development, and interpersonal communication skills, but also help students develop a sensitivity to their audience, and in the process, students assume greater responsibility for their own learning (Barron and Darling-Hammond 2008; Duke 2021). Project-based learning units typically have a final product, presentation, or performance for an authentic audience built into their design. The final performance not only answers the question "Why are we doing this?" but also "Who is this for?"

## They Become Little Versions of Me

Let's revisit Esther's advanced journalism class for another example of authentic audiences. It's two o'clock in the lecture hall. The newspaper has been distributed. Eight students sit on a stage facing fifty of their peers. Several newspapers are spread out in front of them on the floor.

"Let's start," one says. "What'd you think of page one?" Shouting out and over each other, students begin to critique the paper: "There's no dominance on page one." "The caption's wrong." "That column doesn't make sense." "I liked the noodle headline." Two adults sit off to the side of the stage, making comments now and then when there's a pause in the discussion. They interject, "Your audience needs to know which is pro and which is con." "The stress poll was well done." The four students at the front push the action along: "Okay, page two. Comments?"

The way these student editors lead the critique process of their public product—the school newspaper—is impressive. But it took time and training to get there. Sophomore students come into beginning journalism without a clear sense of what it means to critique writing. Esther explains how they develop their skills over time:

> I find that when they first come into class, they don't evaluate at all. So, they come in just as passive listeners and they see a movie, and they're like, "Oh, that was good" or "Oh that was bad." So, I say, "Why was it good?' "Why was it bad?" "Well, I don't know why it was good. It was good because it was a good story." I say, "You can break it down more than that." And it takes a really long time for them to get this whole idea going. I mean, by the time they finish beginning journalism they're beginning to think that way, and in advanced journalism they all think like that, and that's why they tear each other apart, tear the paper apart, and tear the whole thing apart. But nobody takes it personally because it's a way of looking at information and the world.

Esther describes the transformation when students advance as juniors and seniors: "They become little versions of me. They are so critical of the writing. They pick it apart like you wouldn't believe. And I think that's why they learn so much. And I just sit there and orchestrate or watch."

Publishing a student paper has high stakes as well. Your peers are picking it up on their way to class or, more likely these days, reading it on their phones. The paper is both about them and for them. What they write is seen and evaluated by their peers—not just the editors but the entire student body. While a journalism program is often situated as an extracurricular activity in the school, students can use journalism skills across subject areas, whether it's interviewing a family member, writing a review of a book, creating a graph of trends, or composing an op-ed.

In fact, over time the entire English department at Esther's high school adopted the personal interview (or personality feature) as the very first writing assignment of the year. Students interview other students, write up what they learn, and share it with the class. This not only launches their learning about writing, but also contributes to building their class community as they learn about each other.

As Jal Mehta writes in his article arguing for a new grammar of schooling: "Schools are not just where we communicate academic content; they are where we raise our young people. Our current grammar of schooling inhibits much of what we want for those young people" (Mehta 2022). He challenges us, "Why not create a new structure that is consistent with our highest aspirations?"

## Reflection Questions: Authentic Audiences

Here are some questions for reflection focused on developing authentic audiences. If you are a leader who works with teachers, you might have teachers read this chapter and reflect on their current practice or choose one small shift to make this week or this month. If you are a teacher, you might use the questions to reflect on your current practice or identify one question to discuss with your colleagues.

- What is the purpose of the activity, from the student's point of view?
- Who is the audience for students' work?
- How is students' work connected to—or reflective of—their lives and their communities?
- What questions could we ask students to find out what activities would feel authentic and relevant to them?
- Does the task or activity mirror "real life"? Does the task or activity matter or make a difference?
- Who gives feedback to students and how is it shared? Who evaluates the work? Are the criteria for assessment clear?
- What opportunities do students have for practice, revisions, and improvement?

# CHAPTER 5

# Play the Whole Game

*We can ask ourselves when we begin to learn anything: "Do we engage some accessible version of the whole game early and often?"*

—DAVID PERKINS

Esther taught her daughters how to ride a two-wheeler bike when they were only three and four years old. No training wheels, no helmets, no special scooters without pedals. Just two tiny bikes in a large parking lot. She simply broke the process down for them: first just practice balancing, then practice where your feet go. Steering came last. The fearless little ones were off and pedaling within a day.

Very much like teaching someone to ride a bike, Esther broke down journalistic writing into steps for her students. She sequenced the skills of being a good interviewer and helped her students master each component: first coming up with questions, then asking people you don't know for an interview, and learning how to take notes and using a recorder. When they lost their notes or the recorder didn't work, she also let them fail and try again, knowing that they would face the same challenges in the work world and that school was a safe space to practice these real-life skills.

As her program grew, her sophomore students became known as "cubbies" (cub reporters) to the now-experienced juniors and seniors who ran the paper. When computers came on the scene, she paired the cubbies with upper classmen for one-on-one software tutorials. Thirty years later, she still recalls how she shifted her instruction:

> How did I go from a situation where they were dependent, and they were just sitting there waiting for me to tell them what to do? Well, in summary, it was

small steps. And I modeled a lot of the behavior that I wanted them to exhibit. For example, in beginning journalism, when I first arrived, the class was organized around a textbook. And all they did was read the chapter and then take a quiz at the end. My question was, how are they supposed to learn to write? So, I collected the textbooks, moved them back into the book room, and I brought in real newspapers from those free newspaper racks.

Esther's students read articles of all types and brought examples of articles into class as homework. She projected the articles on an overhead screen, and they analyzed them together. "See how the opinion is right up front?" she'd say. Or for a restaurant review, "You've got to have specific prices for the dishes." She led mini workshops on writing effective hooks, she had students go to sports events to write up the games, and she gave them lots and lots of written, detailed feedback on their writing, as an editor would.

So many visitors to her award-winning journalism program were interested in the final product—the newspapers, magazines and news shows. But I wanted to go back the beginning. What kinds of skills, habits, and dispositions did the students need to learn to eventually run the program themselves?

### The Missing Link
Esther had identified a missing link. You can't just throw students into the deep end of writing high quality articles.

She methodically lifted the veil on a set of practices to make the art and the craft of journalism apparent to her students, who were eager to express their opinions, to review a movie they had seen or to write about a basketball game they had attended. One memorable year, a group of advanced students conducted an investigative journalism project that uncovered corruption in their school board.

Esther sums up the importance of this kind of preparation for more independent work:

> There must be a clear pattern for everybody: We're all writing restaurant reviews this week. You need to have a clear view of what you want these kids to write, you have to teach it to them, and then they've got to follow it. Just like what I did today in my English class with the five-paragraph essay. I went through what belongs in an introductory paragraph, what the first sentence says, what the body of it should say, and what the end should say. If you don't put that in there, you haven't done it right.

In addition to helping her students understand the structure of a particular genre of writing, Esther spent a lot of time in the beginning journalism class collaboratively critiquing articles with her students, analyzing both strong and weak models on the overhead screen.

Esther describes the small shifts in her instruction as she supports her students' independence:

I'm *backing out slowly*. I'm giving them skills and then letting them do it, and then I just back out. To a point where in advanced journalism, I'm backed out. I'm gone. That's why I say, "Save all your work" because if you get stuck in advanced journalism you can refer back to all the work you did in beginning journalism. I say, "Don't think I'm gonna run there and hold your hand. You have to hold your own hand."

Her ultimate goal is to help her students play "a junior version" of the whole game, as Harvard University's David Perkins describes it in his book *Making Learning Whole* (2009). She wants her students to become the editors-in-chief, to lead their peers, and run every aspect of the newspaper. Her beginning journalism class prepares them by building their writing skills. By the time they get to advanced journalism, they have a foundation. They understand what a reporter does, how to write, how to conduct interviews, and how to critique their own and other students' pieces.

Teachers often talk about "I do, we do, you do" as short-hand for a gradual release of responsibility from the teacher to the student. And very often the misconception is that this gradual release can happen in just a lesson or a few lessons. But what Esther illustrated for me is that it takes much more time. Sophomores spent a *semester* in beginning journalism learning how to become a junior journalist—not just how to write, but learning what models of excellence look like, exploring the ethics of being a journalist, and practicing citizenship skills like learning how to write an op-ed. She also shows us that if you break complex tasks down and provide clear steps along the way, they can't fail.

## Tricks of the Trade

How do babies learn to play peek-a-boo? Believe it or not, child psychologist and language expert Courtney Cazden was interested in this very question (Cazden 1979). Why? Because it illustrates the teaching-learning dynamic and the gradual release of responsibility from the adult to the child perfectly. Cazden breaks down the sequence for us: First the parent does every part of the game: holding up a blanket, then lowering it for the surprise and the inevitable smile from the baby. Then the parent does just the first part—holding up the blanket—and the baby lowers it. Over time the baby learns to do the whole sequence, lifting the blanket themselves with anticipation and lowering it for that moment of wonder and glee. The surprise never gets old, as many parents of young children will tell you. The parent does this whole process without any training. She just knows that learning involves modeling and a release of responsibility, with a gradual move toward independence.

Very often, when envisioning student-centered learning environments, we skip to the final performance, the published product, and the celebration—or a school newspaper. But equally, or perhaps more importantly, is how we prepare our students to succeed in these culminating performances—how we build their skill sets, their conceptual understandings and knowledge of a field or discipline, how we support their collaboration with others, and how we provide feedback for improvement. These are not only key features of supportive learning environments, but also critical to preparation for college and career.

Every discipline, field, or trade has a set of rules, which is often invisible to learners. A key aspect of teaching in a student-centered, or learner-centered, way is to make those hidden strategies visible, to provide models of exemplary practice, and to examine the models together. Part of teaching is being able to articulate, show, and reveal these "tricks of the trade"—whether the discipline is science, history, math, or English. Educational psychologist, Lee Shulman, called this "pedagogical content knowledge"—that is, not just knowing your discipline, but understanding how to identify the essential content, skills, and strategies and provide scaffolding for learners to enter the field (Shulman 1986). We assume learning is sink or swim—you either "get it" or you don't—but for any complex task, the learner needs things to be broken down so that they can try, receive feedback, and try again, in an iterative process.

Apprenticeship involves an expert breaking down tasks into parts and making their expert strategies visible to the learner. Allan Collins calls apprenticeship in schools "cognitive apprenticeship" because the expert or teacher needs to make their *thinking* visible (Collins 1991). Unlike an apprenticeship to a cobbler or a blacksmith, where the craft is visible in the shoes or metalwork, apprenticing to a subject area relies on an expert explaining their thinking, providing models, and—very often—talking a lot. The expert shares their knowledge, strategies, and insights and supports the learner with feedback and mentorship, with the goal of gradually releasing the responsibility for the learning and the final product to the learner.

What does this look like in the classroom? Collins illustrates cognitive apprenticeship in three content areas: reading, writing, and mathematics. In reading, students engage in discussions about a text, where they practice strategies that good readers use like asking questions, summarizing, and predicting. A teacher can model this in small groups, handing more and more responsibility to the students for the text discussion over time. In writing, a teacher can provide planning cues for students to consider as they write first drafts, which are then posted on cards so that they can eventually use them independently. And in mathematics, a lot of evidence shows that teachers sharing their own process of problem-solving—through thinking aloud as they solve a problem in front of the class—can support students in coming up with their own strategies for problem-solving.

In sum, **apprenticeship** in the classroom involves:

- engaging with and observing **models and exemplars of expert practice**, which can include an expert thinking aloud
- a motivating, **authentic context and a clear purpose**, linking the application of skills to a real-life situation
- a **metacognitive stance** ("let's step back and reflect on what we are learning")
- a **community of practice** and collaboration

- opportunities to practice new skills with **feedback and critique**
- a **gradual release of responsibility** from the teacher to the students

This last step, the gradual release, is often the hardest.

Apprenticeships are not only supportive and engaging, but they are also responsive to where the learner is in their development, as psychologist Howard Gardner explains:

> [Apprenticeships] are often highly motivating; young-sters enter directly into the excitement that surrounds an important, complex, and sometimes mysterious undertaking, where the stakes for success (and the costs of failure) may be high... [They] embody centuries of lore about how to best accomplish the task at hand, and this lore can be invoked or exemplified *at the precise moment when it is needed*, rather than at some arbitrary location in a lecture, text, or syllabus (Gardner 1991, 124, emphasis added).

Ultimately, the end goal of an apprenticeship is student leadership—students taking charge. This involves the teacher ceding control, which is hard and scary. It means stepping to the side, even though it would be easier to do it yourself. And it involves truly understanding your craft so that you can break it down for another. Apprenticeships both mirror what happens before school starts, in the home with a caregiver, and what happens after school ends, in internships or field placements. However, this model is often missing from what comes in the middle—our K–12 schools.

Cognitive development researcher, David Perkins, calls this "playing the whole game":

> We can ask ourselves when we begin to learn anything, do we engage some accessible version of the whole game early and often? When we do, we get what might be called a "threshold experience," a learning experience that gets us past initial disorientation and into the game. From there, it's easier to move forward in a meaningful motivating way. Much of formal education is short on threshold experiences. It feels like learning the pieces of a picture puzzle that never gets put together or learning about the puzzle without being able to touch the pieces. In contrast, getting some version of a whole game close to the beginning makes sense because it gives the enterprise more meaning. You may not do it very well, but at least you know *what you're doing and why you're doing it* (Perkins 2009, 9, emphasis added).

I was drawn to Esther's classroom—and motivated to return week after week to observe what was going on—because I saw how the pieces of the puzzle were all being put together in a meaningful way. I saw student agency and choice, active learning, students becoming experts, and writing for authentic audiences—all in the context of playing the whole game. Students knew what they were doing and why they were doing it. And at the end of the day, they didn't want to leave. Esther was often shooing them out the door to get them home before midnight.

## Building Blocks

When my daughter was eleven, we took her to meet a Jewish educator in our community to explore whether she wanted to have a bat mitzvah. I never had a bat mitzvah myself. It seemed like a lot of work, and I did not have a connection to my synagogue. My daughter did not attend religious school. But I heard about this teacher from a friend of mine who said the ceremony she attended was the most meaningful experience, full of love, music, and a true rite of passage. I was hooked.

After meeting Julie Batz, who in real life was as engaging, warm, and wise as we had heard, we were not entirely surprised when my daughter said "yes" to a year of study. This included learning Hebrew from zero experience, interpreting the Torah, and ultimately leading her community of family and friends in a very detailed, two-hour service. Julie, her mentor and guide through this process, had a steady, warm, and spiritual presence like no one we had ever met. She made the whole experience fun and fascinating with storytelling and full confidence in the tutorial process she had honed over many years. How Mia was going to learn to read Hebrew in a year, not just Hebrew but biblical Hebrew—and not just biblical Hebrew, but Hebrew with only consonants and no vowels, as it was written in the original scrolls—was beyond me. Add to this challenge learning how to *chant* Hebrew according to a series of tropes (a type of cantillation with its own notation system), and the whole venture seemed way beyond what was possible for a twelve-year-old.

But Julie, like Esther, had developed a system that broke down the learning into its component parts. They started with the alphabet, and slowly but surely—over the course of several months—Mia was reading Hebrew, then reading consonants without vowels, then chanting. At the end of the year, she stood in front of us and guided our community in a service that included her interpretation of her assigned portion of the Torah (the first five books of the bible) in a way that made her seem twenty, not thirteen. It was amazing.

Julie had figured out the learning progression toward mastering Hebrew which made the process attainable, step by step. It was almost as though she was pointing out to Mia the best foot holds and hand holds on a climbing rock so that she could accomplish the challenge on her own, but with specific, guided support. Young people are capable of so much more than we can imagine. Julie was also incredibly passionate about her subject, as are all the teachers and teacher educators featured in this book. This passion is infectious. If the teacher is curious, interested, and engaged then the students can get swept up in that wave. The apprenticeship was built on a foundation of relationship, trust, and respect. Julie's confidence in her students and deep care for their success was palpable. Isn't this what we want for all our students—an opportunity to stretch, to learn new skills, to become their best selves, and to share their learning with their community?

For Julie, Esther, and all the teachers in this book, they had to step back and assess the specific building blocks toward successful mastery of the skills and dispositions of a journalist, a leader, a speaker, a business consultant, or a citizen activist. To support students in having experiences that approximate "playing the whole game," we need to have an understanding of the steps that get you from T-ball to little league. As you will see in the next chapter, building a deep understanding of how a student becomes successful as a learner in a discipline or a content area often depends on collaboration with teacher colleagues.

## Reflection Questions: Apprenticeship

Here are some questions for reflection focused on apprenticeship and scaffolding. If you are a leader who works with teachers, you might have them read the chapter and reflect on their current practice or choose one small shift to make this week or this month. If you are a teacher, you might reflect on your current practice or identify one question to discuss with your colleagues.

- What are some ways to make expert practice visible to students?
- How can we model what good scientists/writers/readers/mathematicians/historians do?
- How can we sequence students' learning so that it builds toward real-life performances of understanding?
- How can we create tasks that are building blocks toward "playing the whole game"?

- What opportunities can we provide for students to practice, to fail, and to try again?
- How can we support students' emerging independence and leadership?

# CHAPTER 6

# Teachers at the Center

*One never learns to teach once and for all. It is a continuous, ongoing, constantly deepening process.*

—LEE SHULMAN

"Let's just get through this agenda quickly so we can go home." I overheard this comment from a group of teachers seated at a small table in a fourth grade classroom after school. Clearly tired from a long day, they were eager to get back to their families and homes. When I moved to join their group, I could feel the resistance. My heart sank. My colleagues and I at WestEd had spent months designing what we felt was an engaging discussion protocol for the teachers to learn together.

We thought we had accounted for everything that we know is important to teachers' professional learning: Teachers were in small, grade-level groups, the groups were self-facilitated, and the discussion protocol provided for sharing and reflection on practice. The focus of the discussion was how to implement a new writing curriculum, so the work was relevant and timely. This was the opposite of a "sit-and-get" workshop and the first step in launching ongoing, job-embedded, teacher inquiry projects.

We had hoped that teachers would have productive discussions about successes and challenges in their instruction, in preparation for investigating their own practice. We knew that lesson pacing was the number one thing that teachers new to the *Being a Writer* curriculum typically struggled with. (Remember Caree's story in Chapter 1 when she realized she was talking too much, and her students were running out of time to write?). But we had left out a key ingredient: teacher choice (hello, Agency!). This is like leaving the baking soda out of the cookies. Leave out teacher choice, and motivation will be flat. After the first few rounds of these after-school discussion groups, we surveyed the teachers, and sure enough, the top comment in their feedback was that they wanted to be able to choose the topic their groups focused on.

Not surprisingly, the key components for learner-centered adult learning are no different from student-centered learning: choice and voice (agency), engaging and interactive learning activities (active learning), opportunities to deepen content knowledge (authority), peers to share learning with (authentic audiences), and models of expert instruction with opportunities to practice and receive feedback (coaching/apprenticeship). But "professional development" has looked the same for decades: very often "one shot," day-long workshops with stale box lunches and hardly any time to process—much less apply—the new learning. (Again, teachers as empty vessels to be filled up—sound familiar?)

If you work with teachers in any capacity—administrator, coach, teacher leader—this chapter is especially for you.

## Teachers as Learners

Let's revisit our five As learner-centered framework, but with teachers as the learners. Learner-centered instruction for teachers includes:

- **Teacher Agency**: choice of topic, ownership of the process, and joint goal setting.

- **Active Learning**: collaboration, metacognition, and reflection with practice-focused data collection and continuous improvement processes.
- **Development of Authority**: deep inquiry in content areas and pedagogy and deep understanding of evidence-based practice.
- **Authentic Audiences**: opportunities for making learning public, sharing learning, peer feedback and reenvisioning practice.
- **Apprenticeship**: exemplars of expert teaching practice, coaching, and expert feedback.

These activities involve both a change in practice and a change in mindset. The change in practice is learning together (not by yourself behind your classroom door), reflecting, inquiring, and using data to make small shifts visible. The change in mindset is that evolving as teacher—and as a learner of teaching—is never finished. As my mentor Lee Shulman puts it so elegantly, teaching "is a continuous, ongoing, constantly deepening process" (Shulman 2004, 517).

Learning Forward, the nation's largest professional learning organization, echoes the five As in their professional learning standards, in particular in their focus on "transformational processes," which includes the use of data and evidence to manage change in practice. They recommend that teacher professional learning include immersive learning experiences, book studies, co-teaching, expert coaching and mentoring, peer feedback, and teacher collaboration.

So, how can we help teachers to reflect on their practice and use evidence, so they can see where such small shifts are possible?

One simple way we can support teachers to make small shifts in their instruction is by encouraging them to get to know their students and their students' interests. This can be as straightforward as giving a short survey or as in-depth as conducting empathy interviews (remember Stephanie, who interviewed second grader Don who didn't want to share his writing in Chapter 4?). We can examine current plans and curriculum to see where we might make adjustments to better reflect our students' communities (recall our first story in Chapter 1 about observing the high schoolers giving tacos to their neighbors during their break? And Kai in Chapter 4 who tweaked his GMO lesson?). Students bring with them to school a wealth of experiences, cultures, languages, traditions, and skills.

A small shift might include taking some time to build in peer-to-peer conversations or peer-to-peer feedback on an assignment—or simply having class in an outdoor space. And providing a clear model or exemplar of a final product, with a clear rubric for what success looks like, gets us halfway toward an apprenticeship experience.

## Active Learning: Small Shifts Through Collaboration

Let's return to our story of the reluctant teacher in my discussion group. It turns out that not all the teachers were resistant to having a conversation about successes and challenges in their writing instruction. And over time, with discussion protocols guiding their work—and more choice, of course—the teachers were able to take a step back from their teaching and see what they might try in their classrooms. They brainstormed what change ideas they could test to address their challenges in teaching the new program. We called these discussions "learning huddles" (Austin et al 2018, Austin et al 2022, Bowman & Austin, 2022).

In one learning huddle, a group of third grade teachers decided to focus on writing conferences. Their first challenge was fairly simple. They realized they actually didn't know how many conferences they were holding each week or which kids they were reaching. The curriculum suggested that teachers confer with two to three students per day, but sometimes they only had time for one conference or none. So, the teachers developed a simple conference tracker that allowed them to see how many conferences they were having per week and per day, and which kids they were meeting with. Some teachers were surprised to see they weren't reaching all their kids. And some noticed that the kids who needed more of their help were not getting it.

The next time they met in their learning huddle to review their data (that included who they had met with and how often), they surfaced another problem. While they were now reaching more students, they noticed a new gap in their practice. They didn't have a way to check whether the conference was having the intended outcome. That is, were their students actually *implementing* the writing revisions they had discussed with them? So, the teachers added another two columns to their tracker, one for the "praise point" and one for the "work on" point, so they could circle back with kids on the specific feedback they had provided the next time they met.

None of these were monumental changes to their teaching practice. But through collaboration and discussion with their peers (surfacing challenges and change ideas together) and making aspects of their teaching visible (through the simple data trackers) the teachers were gradually able to move toward instruction that met the needs of each student. They were paying closer attention to their practice by keeping records. They were also becoming more intentional in their teaching. The question they began with (who are we reaching?), gradually evolved to more nuanced questions, making more intentional choices and timely interventions. That intentionality is essential to becoming an effective teacher.

As we built a learner-centered culture with these teams of teachers, we were able to foster collective responsibility for the outcomes, support their continuous learning, and help them to pursue projects that were both sparked by curiosity and informed by disciplined inquiry (Hough et al 2017).

As a recent report from the National Center on Education and the Economy suggests, teacher professional learning should be focused on job-embedded practice with active learning experiences:

Adult learning should only be considered effective when it changes practices for the better... [I]t is fundamental that for teachers' learning to be effective it must include a range of activities connected to their classroom practice... Most adults change their practices not simply from reading and observing others' work, but from combining these passive activities with active collaboration and learning-by-doing. This cycle of learning is consistent with Knowles' five assumptions of adult learning theory: that adults are self-directed learners, they bring a wealth of prior experience to education, they are ready to learn, are problem centered in their learning, and are best motivated by internal factors (Jensen et al 2016).

Although it took some tinkering (and some failures) for us to design the professional learning to reflect these key aspects of adult learning theory, it was exciting to see what shifted when we were able to combine these elements: activities that were self-directed and group-directed, problem-centered, and motivated by what was happening in teachers' own classrooms.

## Teacher Agency: Clear Targets

In our second attempt with facilitating teacher learning huddles, instead of asking all the grade level teams to focus on lesson pacing, we gave them the choice of four evidence-based practices in the form of a "sandbox" of options: daily writing time, engaging students, peer collaboration and writing conferences. Not surprisingly, this went much better. Teachers decided in their groups what to focus on—not only what they needed to improve, but also what they were *interested* in improving.

But, as I illustrated in Chapter 1, learner agency is not only about choice and voice; agency should also include goal setting, a key feature missing from many professional development efforts. We too often see professional learning as a single event as opposed to an iterative process.

So how does a teacher set a goal for her teaching? The nonprofit Center for the Collaborative Classroom, with headquarters in Alameda, California, has come up with a unique approach to individualizing teacher learning. It starts with a brief survey. Teachers reflect on their current practice in teaching phonics, a highly routinized program, and identify specific areas for improvement. Veteran teacher and coach Lindee Witt, an early participant in the Collaborative Coach experience, explains how identifying a focus supports her learning: "I knew what I wanted to work on, and so everything was targeted around that. I was focused on a procedure that you use when students make a mistake that gets students to go back to think about how to fix that mistake."

What happens next? Lindee video records herself teaching the lesson, which she admits is a daunting prospect, even for an experienced teacher like herself, and she reflects on how it went. Then her coach provides some targeted feedback on the video. Here's the catch: Lindee's personalized coach is not in her school, not even in her state. In fact, her coach is in Florida and Lindee is in California. How can this possibly work? Through specific, personalized, individualized feedback—which, by the way, does not take more than an hour or two in total for her coach to provide. Lindee reflects: "I think the coaching was less intrusive and less intimidating because I knew it was something I wanted to work on. It wasn't somebody else's predetermined objective. It was what I needed."

Gina Fugnitto, vice president of implementation at Collaborative Classroom, and one of the developers of this unique coaching method, was stunned by the results: "Usually, when you coach a teacher, you sit side-by-side and you're interrupting in some way—whether with your body language or when you ask a question, or you'll say, 'Let's look at this together.' But in the video, there's nobody there but themselves. What's mind blowing is the self-coaching that happens. You watch them self-coach *themselves*."

The third grade teachers in their writing conferences had a clear target: confer with two to three students a day. Caree with her first graders had a clear target: students will write for fifteen to twenty minutes a day. Lindee wanted to stick to the script instead of jumping in too soon to offer her own correction. Just as the step count in our fitness apps gives us feedback on how many steps we've walked every day, clear targets give us something to shoot for and valuable feedback when we haven't quite hit the mark.

## Authentic Audiences: Public and Shared Learning

Let's consider how our fourth A—authentic audiences—plays out in teacher learning. The Mills Teacher Scholars—now Lead by Learning at Mills College at Northeastern University—has been supporting teachers' shifts in practice for two decades. They started with a simple premise, articulated by founder and teacher educator, Anna Richert:

> One of the most powerful ways to shift the adult learning culture in schools and districts is through public learning. By *making learning public* by design, we acknowledge the uncertainty and complexity inherent in the work of teaching. When teachers go public with the questions they have about their students' learning and then share the data they collect to help answer those questions, learning becomes the centerpiece of powerful teaching (Richert 2012, emphasis added).

The approach that Anna designed, which her colleagues have grown into a national program, starts with sharing problems of practice. Teachers or leaders meet in groups and share their struggles and challenges. In my conversation with Lead by Learning's senior director of programs, Sarah Sugarman (who was also my daughter's incredible second and third grade teacher), she explained with passion and clarity:

> This work is about inquiring into whether your teaching is having the effect you want it to have. It begins with a dilemma or a challenge. Maybe it's, 'I can't

figure out how to reach this kid' or 'I'm confused about what I'm supposed to be teaching.' A leader might wonder, 'How do I help all my educators feel unified around a common goal?' Bringing those uncertainties to the table as the meat of what teachers and leaders are talking about is what we call public learning.

Such a group helped Stephanie, Don's teacher, when he refused to share his writing at the family event. She learned about student interviews as a key source of data to inform her teaching and was able to engage in dialogue with other educators about how to best support him.

Sugarman goes on with conviction:

> Student-centered shifts in practice are most likely to happen when there's a community or a system in place that helps teachers and leaders be change agents. Just like students, educators thrive when they are actively engaged and having meaningful peer-to-peer connections. Like students, they need to feel that there's an authentic audience for their action research. At every level of the system, learning should basically *look the same.* It can have the same essential qualities for educators as it has for kids.

Just as public audiences for students inspire motivation (that is, "someone is actually going to read what I wrote"), public audiences for teacher learning support teacher-centered activities that are collaborative, motivating, and meaningful. They break down the walls of the classrooms so that teachers and leaders can learn from each other.

## Apprenticeship: Giving Up the Rubber Stamp

I recently caught up with our journalism teacher, Esther, twenty-five years after I visited her high school. She hadn't changed a bit. Still straight-talking, suffering no fools, and still passionate about teaching and learning. Now retired from teaching, she speaks all over the globe about her philosophy of teaching and parenting. I asked her to reflect on how she mentored new teachers to teach the journalism students at her high school, and she thought back to her first hire, Paul, who didn't take to her teaching style right away: "He was very controlling. He brought a big red stamp with him that he would stamp on a student's piece, 'OK for publication.' And so, all of the students' work had to go through him." He saw himself as the editor of the newspaper, even though his title was "advisor."

During his first year, Paul observed Esther's classes as an apprentice would. He saw how Esther interacted with her students and how much trust she gave them, particularly the senior editors, who had been elected by their peers. Over time he started to take on some of her approach. Esther describes the change she observed, "He finally let the editors take some of the stage. He moved over slowly. And he gave the kids more control over editing each other's work. He still went over everything. But they moved into a role of having more responsibility. He's 'me' today. And then we hired three more teachers, and they all became clones of me."

What helped Paul to make this change? Esther points to relationships:

The thing that was most interesting to him is how passionate my students were about me and about what I was doing. And he wanted to get in on that. He became good friends with the students and became a mentor. Teachers are often so afraid of being friends with their students. They want to maintain that distance. Initially, he had a really huge barrier, and then he dropped it, and then all the other new teachers dropped it too. But they need a mind shift in order to do it. The first step is for the teacher to *want to do it*. The second step is to do it slowly, little bits at a time.

For Paul, it wasn't a matter of having Esther's approach explained to him and then implementing it. He needed to see it in action, both how she coached her students as well as all the behind-the-scenes work she did to support the students when they needed it. He saw the learning opportunities that were opened by ceding that control. And, by the way, Esther would never say that she gave up all control. A foundation of trust and respect for her students enabled them to thrive, to make mistakes, learn from them and keep going. Today, many of her former students are leaders in their fields.

The new journalism teachers' learning centered on three key aspects: observing an expert in action, receiving one-on-one coaching, and learning together with their peers. Importantly, there was also time for new learning and the underlying sense that it takes time for even small shifts in teaching. Paul spent *a year* observing Esther before he gave up his rubber stamp. It took observing and practicing for his mindset to shift. Anything worth learning takes time. Why do we assume that learning to teach is any different?

My hope is that by reading these stories teachers and teacher educators will better understand what an engaging, motivating learning environment can look like for their students—and for teachers. Don't we all deserve experiences that spark joy in learning?

## Reflection Questions: Teacher-Centered Professional Learning

Here are some reflection questions focused on the design of teacher learning.

- In what ways are teachers given the opportunity to choose their own topics, set goals, collect data for continuous improvement, and reflect on their learning? (Agency)
- How do designs for professional learning engage teachers in iterative cycles of learning and collaboration focused on student-centered practice and student-centered lesson design? Do teachers leave professional learning experiences with specific actions and next steps they will take? (Active Learning)
- How can teachers deepen their knowledge about instruction, evidence-based practice, and pedagogy? How is the professional learning experience sequenced to ensure deep learning over time? (Authority)
- How can we foster a culture of making teaching public in safe spaces for taking risks? What expectations for ongoing learning and sharing—or demonstrations

of learning—are built into the learning culture? (Authentic Audiences)

- What types of coaching, support, or activities make expert teaching visible? How can teaching practices be broken down into smaller, attainable shifts? (Apprenticeship)

# Conclusion

*In 1970 the top three skills required by the Fortune 500 were the three Rs: reading, writing, and arithmetic. In 1999, the top three skills in demand were teamwork, problem-solving, and interpersonal skills. We need schools that are developing these skills.*

—LINDA DARLING-HAMMOND

When I first observed Esther's journalism classroom, I was amazed. How could these students essentially run the program by themselves? But as I took a closer look, I saw there were several ways that Esther was laying the groundwork for the autonomy the advanced students were experiencing. For one, she made sure that her students had cultivated the knowledge, skills and habits of mind in their beginning journalism class—slowly and over a full semester—so they could succeed as more independent leaders in the advanced class. She also set up structures for peer-to-peer support, so she could fade to become the coach on the side.

Educators came from far and wide to see Esther's program, which grew from nineteen students putting out a small newspaper in the eighties to 700 students publishing ten magazines, including an arts and entertainment magazine, sports magazine, and news magazine, in addition to the twenty-eight-page, three-section newspaper, while also running a radio and TV station.

But what intrigued me about Esther's teaching, and what intrigues me about all the stories in this book, is what happened at the beginning and over time and how her students were supported to become "cub reporters" and then full reporters responsible for features and columns. Just as I was curious about how children are supported to play their first game of peek-a-boo, write their first letter, or give their first speech. My hunch was that it had to do with an apprenticeship experience and the process of scaffolding a learner: Let me show you, support you, and provide "trade secrets," all within the context of playing the whole game, with activity, collaboration, and a gradual release of responsibility.

In fact, I became an author apprentice when I chose to participate in the Book Creators' Course in May of 2022. I had always wanted to turn my doctoral dissertation into a publication, but I didn't know how. In our college and graduate classes, for the most part, we research and write for our professors or for a committee—for two, three, four or even more years. When we're done, the work is bound and shelved. (Some students even leave a twenty-dollar bill in the pages to see if anyone ever cracks theirs open!) While I considered writing an academic article, I didn't want my work to stagnate in a stuffy library or be inaccessible behind an online paywall. And I knew that I wanted to write for educators.

I had no idea how to write a book. But each week, the Book Creators' course instructors and editors revealed another piece of the puzzle: Here are the elements of an introduction, here's how to stitch together seemingly disparate stories, here's a detailed checklist for each chapter to make sure you have a complete draft. They drew back the curtain on expert nonfiction writing practice so that I could, as a novice, step-by-step, put together my first book. Along the way, they not only provided these concrete tips and trade secrets, but also a personal coach (a.k.a. an editor) and essential motivational support. They assured us, "You are going to think your work sucks; we all do" and "A good first draft is a done first draft." Other authors in the course were going through the same ups and downs I was experiencing, which meant, depending on the day, feeling alternately inspired and energized or sincerely doubting whether a decent book was ever going to emerge. Being able to empathize and share with each other was key. And what's more satisfying than having something with your name on it that you are proud of? This sticky note on my computer monitor kept me company the whole way: "Whatever is not shared is lost."

Now that I'm at the end of writing my first book, I have a new appreciation for the creative process. Sometimes you are supposed to feel like you are in a pit, and there is no way out. (My family can attest to you that I "quit" this book project at least ten times.) And you will also feel euphoric when that first line for a story comes to you standing in a towel after getting out of the shower. It's messy, confusing, discouraging, and uplifting—just like learning. And for some weird reason, I have the desire to do it all again.

## Small Shifts

You can look at the current state of education in two ways—as a crisis or an opportunity. The headlines these days are pretty dismal, pointing to teacher burn-out, scores of teachers leaving the profession, and students who are not only years behind grade level but also increasingly struggling with mental health issues. These are real and serious issues. But I would argue that we have a moral responsibility to do the best that we can to provide our students with opportunities for learning that reflect what we know about the science of learning, student motivation, engagement, and empowerment to prepare our young people for success in a changing world—through small shifts in their learning environments.

Language is powerful. As teacher educator Deborah Ball points out:

> We are limited by the paucity of language with which to communicate about teaching. While most other languages have a single word for teaching-and-learning that honors the fundamental relational and connected work, English separates this concept into two different words (Ball 2022).

This false separation only furthers the notion of two entities, as opposed to a complex, relational, dynamic interaction. Now I understand why I had such a hard time creating the subtitle for this book. I kept wanting teaching and learning to be one word: student-centered teaching-and-learning.

On the theme of language, look to Lindsey Unified school district in the California central valley where every teacher is called a "learning facilitator" and their students are "learners." Classrooms in Lindsey are "learning environments" (Lindsey Unified School District 2017). Similarly, in their book *Switch: How to Change Things When Change is Hard*, authors Chip and Dan Heath describe how students in Crystal Jones's class are "scholars," and when visitors arrive in their classroom the students say in unison, "A scholar is someone who lives to learn and is good at it!" These young scholars are also expected to share what they learn with their families (authentic audiences).

In addition to paying attention to classroom culture and language, the Heath brothers describe the importance of a clear goal, or a "destination postcard," that is "a vivid picture from the near-term future that shows what could be possible" (Heath & Heath 2010, 76). To that end, what if our language and our destination postcard shifted from entrenched definitions of what a "student" is, to something more twenty-first century? That is, leaders, content experts, content creators, change-makers, and problem-solvers.

Flipping the lens from what the teacher-as-a-learning-facilitator does to a new vision for our learners, let's revisit our student-centered framework with some questions designed to invite conversations among educators, but centering the students:

Students as Leaders (Apprenticeship)

- How can we support students to:
    - gain knowledge, skills, and strategies from the real-world fields and professions they will ultimately enter?
    - take on more leadership and responsibility within their schools and communities?
    - teach their peers and younger students?

Students as Content Creators and Community Change-Makers (Authentic Audiences)

- How can we support students to:

- create, write, publish for a range of audiences across the variety of platforms available to them?
- get feedback from teachers and peers to learn and improve?
- practice, practice, practice in an iterative way (that is, the first draft is never the final draft)?

## Students as Content Experts (Authority and Expertise)

- How can students become experts by:
  - engaging in tasks and lessons that dive deep into content learning?
  - developing critical thinking and research skills?
  - sharing their learning with each other and engaging with their community?

## Students as Problem-Solvers (Activity)

- How can we provide activities, tasks, and units that involve students in:
  - solving complex problems with clear purposes?
  - engaging their minds, hands, hearts, creativity, and social natures?
  - building skills for a changing, uncertain, and increasingly technology-focused, world?

## Students as Empowered Scholars (Agency)

- How can we support students to:
  - choose their own topics, tasks, and products?
  - talk, talk, talk—particularly with each other?
  - set goals and reflect on their learning process?

By giving students agency, choice, and voice we provide them the opportunity to become change-makers in their communities and leaders in their schools, and they will be better prepared for independent learning in college and careers when they leave high school.

## Starting Small

I've been going to a gym to work out for years. The only problem is the gym is in my head. I keep intending to find a great place, suit up in my workout gear, and go regularly to get "fit," but one day I just decided that would never happen. Instead, I started small. I realized I could manage doing a tiny bit of yoga—one sun salutation a day—on my bedroom carpet, right after brushing my teeth in the morning. (Full disclosure, I am sometimes in my pajamas for this). After a few weeks, I decided to add a moon salutation. A few months later, I added some arm weights—not many, just 10 biceps, 10 triceps, etc. Fast forward a few years, and I have a morning routine that includes squats, a plank, and a tree pose. My point is, I needed to start small, and make the shift attainable for me, given my context and my idiosyncrasies. But I now "work out" every day.

I wrote this book because I am optimistic about what we can do for our students and passionate about how learning theory can inform the changes we make. With small shifts in instruction, moving toward student-centered learning is possible and opens new doors of understanding, insight, and joy. Teachers teach because they love to help their students learn. You can make a classroom more student-centered in so many different ways—from providing more choice, to widening the world of audiences who give students feedback on their work. Wouldn't it be nice if we didn't have to answer the question, "But how does this apply to the real world?" What if the question just answered itself?

## Start Shifting

Some coaches and educators debate about whether to support teachers' learning by starting with the practice (that is, learn by doing) or starting with a shift in mindset (that is, teaching is complex, uncertain, and evolving).

Ideally teachers can try out a new practice in a safe space and in collaboration with colleagues, as my examples have shown. But sometimes it's just about a nudge. In that spirit, here are a few ideas for small shifts you can try right away (tomorrow, even!):

- Rather than having your students turn an assignment in to you, have them assess a peer (with a rubric, ideally) (agency).
- Move the field trip from the end of the unit to the middle of the unit and help students bring their learning back from the field trip to a class project (active learning).
- Instead of a lecture or whole class discussion, find a way to support students in doing their own research and leading a small group discussion (authority).
- Provide a few different options for a final project—video, podcast, visual art—and ask students to show

it to one person and get their feedback (authentic audiences).

- Break down the parts of a problem-solving strategy and think out loud as you are doing it (apprenticeship).

An abundance of resources is available on the topic of student-centered teaching. *The Shift to Student Led* by Caitlin Tucker and Katie Novak is an excellent starting place. They provide specific, concrete examples of how to shift some common teacher "workflows" in the class-room: from whole group discussions to small group discussions, from an audience of one to authentic audiences, and from teacher assessment to peer or self-assessment, for example. They provide lessons, slide decks, planning templates, and activities for making these shifts.

My purpose is not to tell you what to do, but to provide a framework and set of concepts or lenses on your practice—perhaps focusing on one or two "As" at a time. For so many of us, we see the destination, but we don't know how to get there. Most important is modeling for students—or for teachers—that we are learners ourselves. We are trying something new, reflecting on how it went, and tweaking it for next time.

## Cultivating Shifts in Practice Together

It takes more than an individual working toward shifts in practice. It takes a community. When I began doing professional learning with teachers, I thought that I needed to be the expert in the room, but as time went on, I made small shifts—through trying out different discussion protocols, reflection activities, and centering the teachers as the authorities in the room. I became the facilitator of learning experiences. But it took listening with my colleagues—really listening—to teachers' lived experiences to understand how to do that work.

I would encourage you to share and reflect on the framework and stories in this book with your colleagues. Whether you work with students or teachers, which parts of the framework do you feel you have strengths in: agency, active learning, authority, authentic audiences, apprenticeship? Where do you want to grow? Host a book club to discuss the questions from one or more chapters. You will find the reflection questions compiled into a handy appendix at the end of this book. Summer is a great time to take a step back and think about your practice. Where could you make a shift to get to know your learners better or to provide more opportunities for them to take the lead in their learning? But ideally, just go ahead and try something small.

What have you got to lose?

# Acknowledgments

I mentioned in my introduction that I wanted to write this book to become a learner again. One of the most valuable aspects of this whole process has been having the secrets of book writing revealed to me though the Book Creators' course. Since starting the course, I have been on a crusade, telling everyone I know—from my therapist to my kids' friends—that "you should write a book!"

But it's not been easy by any means. I want to leave some breadcrumbs of wisdom for my future self, and for anyone else taking the leap into such an endeavor, which has many ups and downs. While I have made a conscious effort to avoid directives in the writing of this book (you must, you should), I'm going to give myself permission to share some advice and, in the process, thank my amazing supporters.

Notes to my future self with a whole lot of gratitude to my colleagues and supporters:

- Find early champions and cheerleaders for your work (thank you, Pam Fong!).

- Share your struggles. (Thank you, Mia, for the twelve encouraging sticky notes you left for me on my desk before you went back to college. Some of my favorites: "Write bad stuff," "Who cares?" and "Passion projects are not always pleasurable.")
- Ask for advice when you are stuck. (Thank, you Molly, for reminding me to "Find the llamas.")
- Post helpful reminders of your "why." (Thank you, Aimee Evans, author of *Student Centered School Improvement*, for this sticky note on my computer screen: "Whatever is not shared is lost.")
- Get a coach or two. (Thank you to my editors, Angela Ivey and Megan Hart, for your wise counsel and to Book Creators' course instructors, Shanna Heath and Eric Koester, and all of the good folks at New Degree Press who help to birth so many great books.)
- Seek stories. (A huge thank you to all the teachers and educators who took the time to share your stories with me: Esther Wojcicki, Susan Levenson, Vickie Lock, Nancy Gerzon, Caree Walker, Jess Gribbon, Sofi Frankowski, Pam Fong, Natalie Gale, Kai Akana, Jonathan Boxerman, Ron Berger, Stephanie Vollmer, Sarah Sugarman, Lindee Witt, and Gina Fugnitto.)
- Cultivate supportive colleagues (Thank you, Susan Mundry, Pam Fong, and Darl Kiernan for your close read of the manuscript! Thanks to my WestEd colleagues for pointing me in the direction of some fabulous educators.)
- Keep in touch with your favorite teachers. They will always have more wisdom to share. (Looking at you, Esther Wojcicki and Lee Shulman!)

- Talk with fellow authors because they really know what you are going through. (Special shout out to my amazing parents and my staunchest supporters, Susan J. Austin, author of *The Bamboo Garden* and *Drawing Outside of the Lines* and Michael J. Austin, author of more books on social work management than I can list as well as an inspiring, unauthorized autobiography, *Connecting the Dots*.)
- Choose a supportive mate and life partner who gives great shoulder massages and never wavers in his confidence that you can do anything you set your mind to. (Love you, J!)
- Perhaps most important: Listen to your creative urges and what inspires you. Give yourself permission to act on those creative sparks, no matter how *really* rough your rough drafts may seem.

# Small Shifts:
# Reflection Questions

These reflection questions can be used for professional learning or a facilitated book study—either before reading the book or after reading the book. A coach or facilitator might just focus on one set of questions as a focal point or have teachers self-reflect individually in a practice audit and then discuss their answers together. The last set of questions is for facilitators of professional learning and focused on designing teacher-centered learning experiences.

## Student-Centered Teaching

### Agency
- Who is involved in choosing the topics of study?
- Who sets the learning goals and evaluates progress toward those goals?
- Who is doing most of the talking in the room?
- Who is doing most of the work in the learning activities?
- Who gets the opportunity to lead the learning?

## Active Learning

- What is the purpose of the task, lesson, or unit?
- How well does the task, lesson, or unit purpose align to learning goals for students?
- How can students be invited to engage socially and collaborate with each other?
- What are some authentic and engaging "minds-on" problems students can tackle that require them to transfer their learning from one situation to another?
- How can the learning experience involve "hands on" activities in visual arts, drama, dance or movement, engineering, design, or technology?

## Authority

- How can we support students to become experts? How can we step back as the expert, so students can step forward?
- How do the patterns of talk, the nature of assignments, and the intended audiences for student work reflect who is the authority in the room?
- In what ways can going deeper into content also support students' development of essential academic skills (reading, writing, critical thinking)?
- How can we build in opportunities for metacognition and reflection in learning tasks and lessons?
- What kinds of individual and group learning tasks can support students as they develop their knowledge and authority?

## Authentic Audiences

- What is the purpose of the activity, from the student's point of view?
- Who is the audience for students' work?
- How is students' work connected to—or reflective of—their lives and their communities?
- What questions could we ask students to find out what activities would feel authentic and relevant to them?
- Does the task or activity mirror "real life"? Does the task or activity matter or make a difference?
- Who gives feedback to students, and how is it shared? Who evaluates the work? Are there clear criteria for assessment?
- What opportunities do students have for practice, revisions, and improvement?

## Apprenticeship

- What are some ways to make expert practice visible to students?
- How can we model what good scientists/writers/readers/mathematicians/historians do?
- How can we sequence students' learning, so it builds toward real-life performances of understanding?
- How can we create tasks that are building blocks toward "playing the whole game"?
- What opportunities can we provide for students to practice, to fail, and to try again?
- How can we support students' emerging independence and leadership?

## Teacher-Centered Professional Learning

For educators who work with teachers, here are some reflection questions focused on the design of professional learning experiences.

- In what ways are teachers given the opportunity to choose their own topics, set goals, collect data for continuous improvement, and reflect on their learning? (Agency)
- How do designs for professional learning engage teachers in iterative cycles of learning and collaboration around student-centered practice and student-centered lesson design? Do teachers leave professional learning experiences with specific actions and next steps they will take? (Active Learning)
- How can teachers deepen their knowledge about instruction, evidence-based practice, and pedagogy? How is the professional learning design sequenced to ensure deep learning over time? (Authority)
- How can we foster a culture of making teaching public in safe spaces for taking risks? What expectations for ongoing learning and sharing or demonstrations of learning are built into the learning culture? (Authentic Audiences)
- What types of coaching, support or activities make expert teaching visible? How can teaching practices be broken down into smaller, attainable shifts? (Apprenticeship)

# References

## Introduction

Barron, Brigid and Linda Darling-Hammond. 2008. *Teaching for Meaningful Learning: A review of research on inquiry-based and cooperative learning.* George Lucas Foundation.

Carver-Thomas, Desiree. 2022. "Teacher Shortages Take Center Stage." *Learning Policy Institute* (blog), February 9, 2022. https://learningpolicyinstitute.org/blog/teacher-shortages-take-center-stage.

Condliffe, Barbara, Janet Quint, Mary Visher, Michael Bangser, Sonia Drohojowska, Larissa Saco, and Elizabeth Nelson. 2017. "Project-Based Learning: A Literature Review." Working paper, MDRC, October 2017. https://files.eric.ed.gov/fulltext/ED578933.pdf.

Dewey, John. 1916. *Democracy and Education: An Introduction to the Philosophy of Education.* New York: The Free Press.

Henry, Kimberly L., Kelly E. Knight, and Terence P. Thornberry. 2011. "School Disengagement as a Predictor of Dropout,

Delinquency, and Problem Substance Use During Adolescence and Early Adulthood." *Journal of Youth and Adolescence* 41, no. 2: 156–166. https://doi.org/10.1007/s10964-011-9665-3.

Moeller, Julia, Marc A. Brackett, Zorana Ivcevic, and Arielle E. White. 2020. "High School Students' Feelings: Discoveries from a Large National Survey and an Experience Sampling Study." *Learning and Instruction* 66, no. 101301. https://doi.org/10.1016/j.learninstruc.2019.101301.

Stringer, Kate. 2018. "Only Half of Students Think What They're Learning in School Is Relevant to the Real World, Survey Says." *The74million.org.* December 11, 2017. https://www.the74million.org/article/only-half-of-students-think-what-theyre-learning-in-school-is-relevant-to-the-real-world-survey-says/.

Will, Madeline. 2022. "Teacher Job Satisfaction Hits an All-Time Low." *Education Week.* April 26, 2022. https://www.edweek.org/teaching-learning/teacher-job-satisfaction-hits-an-all-time-low/2022/04.

YouthTruth. 2017. "Learning From Student Voice: Are Students Engaged?" *YouthTruth Student Survey.* https://youthtruth-survey.org/wp-content/uploads/2022/10/P21-VERSION-LFSV_Student_Engagement_FINAL-P21-version-2.pdf.

## Chapter 1: Follow the Student

Austin, Kimberlee. 2000. "Coaching as a Metaphor for Teaching in a Community of Practice." 2000. PhD diss., Stanford University. https://searchworks.stanford.edu/view/4516855.

Graham, Steve, Alisha Bollinger, Carol Booth Olson, Catherine D'Aoust, Charles MacArthur, Deborah McCutchen and Natalie Olinghouse. 2012. *Teaching Elementary School students to be Effective Writers: A Practice Guide* (NCEE 2012-4058). Washington, DC: National Center for Education Evaluation and Regional Assistance, Institute of Education Sciences, U.S. Department of Education. https://ies.ed.gov/ncee/wwc/Docs/PracticeGuide/wwc_writingpg_summary_092314.pdf.

Lin-Siegler, Xiaodong, Carol S. Dweck, and Geoffrey L. Cohen. 2016. "Instructional Interventions that Motivate Classroom Learning." *Journal of Educational Psychology* 108, no. 3 (April): 295-299. https://psycnet.apa.org/fulltext/2016-15978-001.html.

Pink, Daniel H. 2009. *Drive: The Surprising Truth About What Motivates Us*. New York: Riverhead Books.

Pintrich, Paul R. 2003. "A Motivational Science Perspective on the Role of Student Motivation in Learning and Teaching Contexts." *Journal of Educational Psychology,* 95: 667–686. https://doi.org/10.1037/0022-0663.95.4.667.

Wojcicki, Esther. 2019. *How to Raise Successful People: Simple Lessons for Radical Results*. Boston, New York: Houghton Mifflin Harcourt.

Wojcicki, Esther and Lance Izumi. 2015. *Moonshots in Education: Launching Blended Learning in the Classroom*. San Francisco: Pacific Research Institute.

## Chapter 2: Learn by Doing

Barron, Brigid, and Linda Darling-Hammond. "Teaching for Meaningful Learning: A Review of Research on Inquiry-based and Cooperative Learning." *Edutopia: The George Lucas Educational Foundation*, (2008). https://files.eric.ed.gov/fulltext/ED539399.pdf.

Cantor, Pamela, David Osher, Juliette Berg, Lily Steyler, and Todd Rose. 2018. "Malleability, Plasticity, and Individuality: How Children Learn and Develop in Context." *Applied Developmental Science* 23, no. 4: 307-337. https://www.tandfonline.com/doi/full/10.1080/10888691.2017.1398649.

Cohen, Elizabeth G., and Rachel Lotan. 2014. *Designing Groupwork: Strategies for the Heterogeneous Classroom*. New York: Teachers College Press.

Darling-Hammond, Linda, Lisa Flook, Channa Cook-Harvey, Brigid Barron, and David Osher. 2019. "Implications for Educational Practice of the Science of Learning and Development." *Applied Developmental Science* 24, no. 2: 97-140. https://doi.org/10.1080/10888691.2018.1537791.

Gardner, Howard. 1985. *Frames of Mind: The Theory of Multiple Intelligences*. New York: Basic Books, Inc.

Goe, Laura, and Leslie M. Stickler. 2018. "Teacher Quality and Student Achievement: Making the Most of Recent Research." *National Comprehensive Center for Teacher Quality*. Accessed December 17, 2022. https://files.eric.ed.gov/fulltext/ED520769.pdf.

Mehta, Jal, and Sarah Fine. 2019. *In Search of Deeper Learning: The Quest to Remake the American High School*. Cambridge: Harvard University Press.

Mehta, Jal. 2022. "Possible Futures: Toward a New Grammar of Schooling." *Kappan* 103, *no.5*, (February). Accessed December 17, 2022. https://kappanonline.org/possible-futures-new-grammar-of-schooling-mehta/.

## Chapter 3: Pass the Mic

Aronson, Elliott, and Shelley Patnoe. 1997. *The Jigsaw Classroom: Building Cooperation in the Classroom*. New York: Longman.

Brown, Ann L., and Joseph C. Campione. 1990. "Communities of Learning and Thinking, or A Context By Any Other Name." *Contributions to Human Development,* 21: 108–126. https://doi.org/10.1159/000418984.

Brown, Ann L. 1997. "Transforming Schools into Communities of Thinking and Learning About Serious Matters." *American Psychologist,* 52, no. 4: 399–413. https://doi.org/10.1037/0003-066X.52.4.399.

Brown, Ann L., Doris Ash, Martha Rutherford, Kathryn Nakagawa, Ann Gordon, and Joseph C. Campione. 1997. "Distributed Expertise in the Classroom." In *Distributed Cognitions: Psychological and Educational Considerations,* edited by Gavriel Salomon. Cambridge: Cambridge University Press.

Duke, Nell, Anne-lise Halvorsen, Stephanie L. Stracan, Jihyun Kim, and Spyros Konstantopoulos. 2021. "Putting PjBL to the Test: The Impact of Project-Based Learning on Second Graders' Social Studies and Literacy Learning and Motivation in Low-SES School Settings." *American Educational Research Journal*, 58, no. 1 (February 2021): 160–200. https://doi.org/10.3102/0002831220929638.

Education Endowment Foundation. 2021. "Teaching and Learning Toolkit: An Accessible Summary of Education Evidence." Accessed January 28, 2023. https://educationendowment-foundation.org.uk/education-evidence/teaching-learning-toolkit.

Halvorsen, Anne-lise, and Nell Duke. 2017. "Projects That Have Been Put to the Test." *Edutopia* (blog), *George Lucas Educational Foundation*. June 20, 2007. https://www.edutopia.org/article/projects-have-been-put-test-anne-lise-halvorsen-nell-duke.

National Research Council. 2000. *How People Learn: Brain, Mind, Experience, and School: Expanded Edition*. Washington DC: National Academies Press.

## Chapter 4: Publish to the World

Barron, Brigid, and Linda Darling-Hammond. "Teaching for Meaningful Learning: A Review of Research on Inquiry-based and Cooperative Learning." *Edutopia: The George Lucas Educational Foundation*, (2008). https://files.eric.ed.gov/fulltext/ED539399.pdf

Bennett, Judith, Fred Lubben, and Sylvia Hogarth. 2007. "Bringing Science to Life: A Synthesis of the Research Evidence on the Effects of Context-Based and STS Approaches to Science Teaching." *Science Education* 91, no. 3 (May 2007): 347–370. https://doi.org/10.1002/sce.20186

Boxerman, Jon. 2022. "Brokering Knowledge in Diverse Classrooms: How Can Teachers Attune to Students' Cultures?" *Next Gen Science, WestEd* (blog). July 13, 2022. https://ngs.wested.org/brokering_knowledge/.

Bruning, Roger, Gregory Schraw, and Monica Norby. 2011. *Cognitive Psychology and Instruction (5th ed.)*. New York: Pearson.

Duke, Nell, Anne-lise Halvorsen, Stephanie L. Stracan, Jihyun Kim, and Spyros Konstantopoulos. 2021. "Putting PjBL to the Test: The Impact of Project-Based Learning on Second Graders' Social Studies and Literacy Learning and Motivation in Low-SES School Settings." *American Educational Research Journal*, 58, no. 1 (February 2021): 160–200. https://doi.org/10.3102/0002831220929638.

Gay, Geneva. 2018. *Culturally Responsive Teaching: Theory, Research, and Practice (Multicultural Education Series) 3rd Edition*. New York: Teachers College Press.

Gebre, Engida H., and Joseph L. Polman. 2020. "From 'Context' to 'Active Contextualization': Fostering Learner Agency in Contextualizing Learning Through Science News Reporting." *Learning, Culture and Social Interaction* 24 (March 2020). https://doi.org/10.1016/j.lcsi.2019.100374.

McTighe, Jay. 2021. "It's Time for Curriculum Mapping 3.0." *Solution Tree Blog* (blog). March 2, 2021. https://www.solution-tree.com/blog/its-time-for-curriculum-mapping-3-0/.

Mehta, Jal. 2022. "Possible Futures: Toward a New Grammar of Schooling." *Kappan* 103, no.5 (February 2022): 54-57. https://kappanonline.org/possible-futures-new-grammar-of-schooling-mehta/.

Nelson-Barber, Sharon, Zanette Johnson, Jonathan Boxerman, & Matt Silberglitt. 2022. "Using Context-Adaptive Indigenous Methodologies to Address Pedagogical Challenges in Multicultural Science Education." In *International Handbook of Research on Multicultural Science Education,* edited by Mary M. Atwater, 711-737. Springer International Publishing.

November, Alan. 2017. "Write for My Teacher, or Publish to The World?" *November Learning (blog)*. February 10, 2017. https://novemberlearning.com/article/write-teacher-publish-world/.

Priniski, Stacey J., Cameron A. Hecht, and Judith H. Haracklewicz. 2018. "Making Learning Personally Meaningful: A New Framework for Relevance Research." *The Journal of Experimental Education*, 86, no. 1 (October 2017): 1-19. DOI:1 0.1080/00220973.2017.1380589.

Vollmer, Stephanie. 2019. "Listen to Teach, Partner to Learn." *Lead by Learning* (blog). August 21, 2019. https://weleadbylearning.org/2019/08/21/listen-to-teach-partner-to-learn/.

## Chapter 5: Play the Whole Game

Cazden, Courtney. 1979. "Peekaboo as an Instructional Model: Discourse Development at Home and at School." Papers and Reports on Child Language Development, no. 17, Stanford University, California, Department of Linguistics. https://eric.ed.gov/?id=ED191274.

Collins, Allan. 1991. "Cognitive Apprenticeship: Making Thinking Visible." *The American Educator* (Winter 1991). American Federation of Teachers. https://www.aft.org/ae/winter1991/collins_brown_holum.

Gardner, Howard. 1991. *The Unschooled Mind: How Children Think and How Schools Should Teach.* New York: BasicBooks.

Shulman, Lee. 1986. "Those Who Understand: Knowledge Growth in Teaching." *Educational Researcher*, 15, no. 2 (February): 4-14. https://www.jstor.org/stable/1175860?origin=JSTOR-pdf.

Perkins, David. 2010. *Making Learning Whole: How Seven Principles of Teaching Can Transform Education.* New Jersey: John Wiley & Sons.

## Chapter 6: Teachers at the Center

Austin, Kim, Alicia Bowman, Marianne Justus, Sola Takahashi, Darl Kiernan, and Pamela Fong. 2022. *Learning Huddles: Design and Facilitation Tips.* San Francisco, CA: WestEd. https://www.wested.org/wp-content/uploads/2023/02/Learning-Huddles_Facilitation-Tips_FINAL.pdf.

Austin, Kim, Darl Kiernan, Sola Takahashi. 2018. "Using Learning Huddles to Improve Teaching and Learning." Regional Educational Laboratory West at WestEd, September 25, 2018. https://ies.ed.gov/ncee/edlabs/regions/west/relwestFiles/pdf/Using-Learning-Huddles-for-Teaching-and-Learning-Slides.pdf.

Bowman, Alicia, and Kim Austin. 2022. *Facilitating Improvement Professional Learning Modules.* San Francisco, CA: WestEd. https://www.wested.org/facilitating-improvement-in-teacher-practice/

Darling-Hammond, Linda, Maria H. Hyler, and Madelyn Gardner. 2017. *Effective Teacher Professional Development.* Palo Alto, CA: Learning Policy Institute. https://learningpolicyinstitute.org/sites/default/files/product-files/Effective_Teacher_Professional_Development_REPORT.pdf.

Hough, Heather, Jason Willis, Alicia Grunow, Kelsey Karusen, Sylvia Kwon, Laura Mulfinger, and Sandra Park. 2017. *Continuous Improvement in Practice.* Pace: Policy Analysis for California Education. https://weleadbylearning.org/wp-content/uploads/2017/09/CI-in-Pratice.pdf.

Jensen, Ben, Julie Sonnemann, Katie Roberts-Hull and Amélie Hunter. 2016. *Beyond PD: Teacher Professional Learning in High-Performing Systems.* Washington, DC: National Center on Education and the Economy. https://weleadbylearning.org/wp-content/uploads/2017/09/BeyondPDDec2016.pdf.

Learning Forward. 2022. *Standards for Professional Learning.* Learning Forward.

Richert, Anna Ershler. 2012. *What should I do? Confronting Dilemmas of Teaching in Urban Schools.* New York: Teachers College Press.

Shulman, Lee. 2004. *The Wisdom of Practice: Essays on Teaching, Learning and Learning to Teach.* San Francisco: Jossey-Bass.

## Conclusion

Ball, Deborah. 2022. "Possible Futures: Coming to Terms With the Power of Teaching." *Kappan,* 103, no. 7 (April 2022): 51-55. https://kappanonline.org/possible-futures-power-of-teaching-ball/.

Heath, Dan, and Chip Heath. 2010. *Switch: How to Change Things when Change Is Hard.* New York: Random House.

Lindsey Unified School District. 2017. *Beyond Reform: Systemic Shifts Toward Personalized Learning.* Bloomington, IN: Marzano Research.

Tucker, Caitlin R., and Katie Novak. 2022. *The Shift to Student-Led: Reimagining Classroom Workflows with UDL and Blended Learning.* San Diego: IMPress.

Made in United States
Troutdale, OR
10/22/2024

24035911R00082